THE RUGBY ABSTRACT

Unifying Rugby Union and Rugby League into One Sport

Mark Campbell

Published in Australia in 2020 by Barcy Publishing

Email: barcypublishing@gmail.com

© Mark Campbell 2020

The moral right of the author has been asserted.

All rights reserved.

No part of this publication may be reproduced, stored in a retrieval system, or transmitted in any form or by any means, electronic, mechanical, photocopying, recording, or otherwise, without prior written permission from the author.

ISBN 9780648902805 (paperback)

A catalogue record for this book is available from the National Library of Australia

Disclaimer

The author has made every effort to ensure the accuracy of the information within this book was correct at the time of publication. The author does not assume and hereby disclaims any liability to any party for any loss, damage or disruption caused by errors or omissions, whether such errors or omissions result from accident, negligence, or any other cause.

For people who hold an imagination.
Don't let the crowd grind you down.

Contents

Introduction   1

SECTION ONE – Rationale
   Chapter 1 – My Connection to the Game   5
   Chapter 2 – Inspiration for Change   7
   Chapter 3 – Rugby's History   11
   Chapter 4 – Why League and Union Should Merge   13
   Chapter 5 – Challenging Natural Prejudices   16

SECTION TWO – The Rules of a United Rugby Game
   Chapter 6 – The Similarities Between the Two Codes   21
   Chapter 7 – The Differences Between the Two Codes   33
   Chapter 8 – The Officials   57
   Chapter 9 – Domestic Rugby Competitions   67
   Chapter 10 – International Rugby   98
   Chapter 11 – Climbing the Mountain   103
   Chapter 12 – The Champions   105

Conclusion   107
Recommended Reading List   111
Acknowledgements   113
About the Author   115

Introduction

In order to determine the world's best rugby nation, I believe it is fundamental for the sports of Rugby Union and Rugby League to be merged into one sport. By providing readers with an understanding of rugby's unique history and culture, I have challenged the natural prejudices that currently exist between the two games. In addressing misconceptions, I have presented an opportunity to provide a platform from which the world's best rugby players (of either code) can compete on a level playing field against each other. Within this book, I provide a breakdown of all the similarities between the fifteen and thirteen player versions of the game in order to highlight how much each sport has in common with the other. At the same time, I acknowledge that there are vast differences in the rules between League and Union.

Moreover, by deconstructing the rules and aspects of officialdom, I have revealed a united form of the game. On top of this, I have addressed the competition structures of the National Rugby League, Super Rugby, English Super League, English Premiership and the Top 14 and Pro 14 and, in doing so, have provided an indication of how fans and players can be brought along on the journey. Additionally, to better clarify my suggested changes, I have adopted a targeted questions and response format to help showcase the recommended ideas. Furthermore, I have expanded on these concepts by using hypothetical competition tables and season structures to offer a concept of what a unified future might embody for a single form of rugby. As well as a discussion of the domestic competitions, I have reviewed the international rugby scene that encompasses the World Cup and the British and Irish Lions tours.

Within this book, I consider the arguments that have plagued the two codes for the last one hundred and twenty-five-plus years but then move on to present a united way forward. Ultimately, both codes of rugby are considered in order to provide the necessary balance for an equitable and balanced example of a single game. Overall, within this book, I have proposed a possible solution for ending the conflict between the two codes in order to unify the sport of rugby as one game.

SECTION ONE

Rationale

CHAPTER 1

My Connection to the Game

I was born in Sydney but grew up in country New South Wales in Australia. Rugby League was the only sport of choice for a kid growing up in this part of the country in the 1980s. Everyone I knew enjoyed the footy but, for me, it was something different. It took on a new life form – following the game and supporting the South Sydney Rabbitohs became a passion, a way of life and something that has stuck with me to this very day.

In my junior years, I played Rugby League. I started in the back row, then in my teens shifted to the wing – even though I was growing, getting fat and was too big to be stuck out on the wing. The reason I stayed on the wing was simple – I hated tackling. Then, as I matured, I moved back into the forwards and, in my later years of high school, I played in the Prop, Second Row position … in the reserves team. Yes, I was no athlete, but I was still very much a fan of the game.

Next, skip forward twenty years and (at the age of 36) for a short season, I played Rugby Union. For the first two games, I was placed back out on to the wing and played five minutes in the first game and then an astonishing two minutes in the next. Yes, I told you. I am definitely not an athlete! In fact, so talented am I that when the next couple of teams arrived short of players, I was transferred onto the other team. To this day, I remain proud of my rugby feats – a try and three try saves (two from tackles and one from an intercept).

Regardless of my lack of skill, I have played both sports and, as such, can appreciate and respect the toughness of the contest in both codes.

CHAPTER 2

Inspiration for Change

With my junior years filled with feats of Rugby League, it was not until the 1991 Rugby Union World Cup that I had any notion that Rugby Union existed. Furthermore, the idea that there was this 'code war' between Rugby League and Rugby Union did not enter my consciousness until just before the 1995 Rugby Union World Cup. At first, I watched the Rugby Union World Cup in 1995 with slight interest, too young to understand and comprehend the relevance of South Africa's hosting and inclusion of the event. Still, to a young Australian, the sight of Jonah Lomu had me hooked.

His feats during that World Cup had me on the edge of my seat. Where did this man come from and why was he not a Rugby League player? As a young man, I thought that Rugby League encompassed all the best players. Remember, this was around the time of Rugby Union's transition into a professional game. In the end, there were only a couple of disappointments from a neutral observer as South Africa went on to claim a famous victory. The first was that the final – although thrilling – went without a try (something almost unheard of in an Australian Rugby League game). The second was a point I have attempted to argue (but failed every time) since the Springbok lifted the trophy to be announced the best rugby team in the world. These words reverberated throughout my being and from this tournament, the seed was planted in my mind. From this point I questioned – *How can they be the best team in the world when they have not beaten the Australian Kangaroos?*

Please do not misunderstand my objection. When the Australian Kangaroos win Rugby League World Cups, the same announcement is made and, as I have become older, I scoff at such a notion. In 2013, the Australian Kangaroos won the Paul Barrière Trophy defeating the New Zealand Kiwis and were declared World Champions. Two years later, the New Zealand All Blacks lifted the William Web Ellis trophy with a victory over the Australian Wallabies and were declared World Champions. From this, I would tell my friends, "Australia and New Zealand are the world's best rugby nations, but our best still have not beaten their best."

Naturally, my friends would roll their eyes.

The trigger that drove home the point around addressing the rugby divide focused more on New Zealand. Call it bias due to geography and culture as an Australian, but the fact is undeniable; since the 1980s, for the most part, the New Zealand All Blacks have been the most dominant Rugby Union team on the planet. At the same time, in Rugby League, the Australian Kangaroos have been the superior force. I make this statement with no disrespect intended for all other rugby playing nations.

I decided to pose the following questions to my Rugby League and Rugby Union loving friends:

1. *How good would it be to see the Australian Kangaroos play the New Zealand All Blacks?*
2. *Who do you think would win?*

Chapter 2 – Inspiration for Change

3. *Would you watch this game?*

The answers were almost always the same. Everyone asked would muse over it and then agree that it would be an awesome game to watch. However, there was an apparent problem: what rules would they play under? For the rules would determine the winner. If it was League, the response favoured the Kangaroos. If the game was played under Union rules, the All Blacks had the vote. Yes, on occasion, national bias crept in. However, for the most part, the response was: the winner would be determined by the rules played.

For the record, there was no doubt about the response to the last question. Without fail, everyone I asked answered that they would watch the match.

Q. *If such an event were to be so popular, why has it not yet happened?*

For this question, there is a multitude of answers. They stretch from lack of free time, payment, concern for injury and, for some people, a lack of interest. Many objections are legitimate – how would the competitions of League and Union work and be adjusted? For example, in Europe, Rugby Union is played in winter whereas League in the United Kingdom is played during the summer months.

There is no doubt that there are many obstacles that would stop such a unification of the sport. However, only under a united form of rugby can people really begin to answer the question: Which nation is the greatest at the sport of rugby?

I did once broach the subject of a mixed match with members of the rugby club in my local community. Their response was at best lukewarm. The answer I received was much along the following lines: "What benefit does it bring us? What if we get injured in a meaningless game?"

This response proved my lack of skills in persuasion. It also revealed either a lack of foresight or desire for change by those who play the sport. I was thankful that it was not a matter of League and Union bias. This rejection improved my understanding of the obstacles; however, it did not and has not since altered my belief that a unified rugby is the best way forward for both codes.

Ultimately, when I have discussed the options of a merged code of rugby, or of a mixed game which included set elements of both sports (League or Union), I am always met with instant rejection. I recognise it may be the way my brain is wired but I have never been fearful of the unknown. I have grown more cautious as the years have passed but never afraid. This way of thinking and viewing the world allows me to process challenges and to make judgements on the validity of such challenges. Unifying the sport of rugby is, in my opinion, an extremely worthy challenge and one that can be overcome and accomplished. I want to see Australian Rugby League players (who are the best rugby athletes in Australia) be appropriately recognised for their worth on the international stage. Lastly, I want the argument and bigotry that currently exists between the two codes to stop.

Thus, I hope this explains my reasoning for attempting to reconcile the two games. I hope you can appreciate an honest attempt on the part of a Rugby League tragic to try to end the divide and to provide an option that could lead the two codes to come together as one – a unified sport of rugby.

CHAPTER 3

Rugby's History

When rugby broke away from the Football Association and crafted its own set of rules, the game exploded in popularity, especially in the north of England. It was due to this growth of popularity that a contrast between the values of fans, players and administrators developed. In the north of England, players were wanting compensation for injuries that occurred during play to offset any time lost at work whereas, for club officials located in the wealthier southern end of England, any payment was considered a form of professionalism. So, as tensions escalated between the clubs based in the working towns of the north (seeking fair compensation) and the clubs of the south (holding onto the ideals of amateurism), there was a split in the game. In this way, since Rugby League's inaugural season in 1895, there have been two forms of rugby.

Rugby's popularity was not confined to English shores. The game spread as far as the British Empire and, as such, rugby became a sport that was played globally. However, it was in the nations of New Zealand and South Africa where rugby became the dominant form of 'football', while in New South Wales and Queensland in Australia, rugby trumped Australian Rules for supremacy. Yet, the class divide followed the sport to the Australian shores where the game once again sought to financially compensate their players. The same conflict around working values and the concept of the amateur game erupted and, once more, a fracture occurred in rugby. Rugby League in Australia began in 1908 and, within ten years, was the dominant rugby code in Australia. Although the sport of Rugby League did take place across the ditch in New Zealand, it did not explode in popularity as it did in Australia.

From such humble beginnings, both sports grew. On a global level, Rugby Union cemented itself as an amateur sport, while Rugby League spread into France prior to the outbreak of World War Two and into other areas where Rugby Union dominated. Nevertheless, the two sports held contrasting values that were quickly highlighted by the rule changes and the administration of the two codes. Rugby League reduced the number of players and changed its rules to cater to a paying public, while Rugby Union maintained tradition and attempted to avoid professionalism. From this divide, animosity between the sports grew and the separation of the amateur game and the professional game lasted for a hundred years – until, in 1995, Rugby Union voted to become a professional sport.

Despite, the era of amateurism coming to an end, the two sports have remained divided. Rugby Union and Rugby League have continued as rivals with each sport always seeking a pathway to gain an advantage and to dominate the other code. And, unless the two games find a way to come together, this is how it will always be.

CHAPTER 4

Why League and Union Should Merge

The seed that was planted in my young mind during the 1995 Rugby Union World Cup has grown. And with the All Blacks domination over the Union code and with the Kangaroos domination over League, I feel now, more so than ever before, that a united code is the way forward.

Without doubt, Rugby League provides the best rugby athletes Australia has to offer. This fact does not diminish the feats of the Australians who have represented the Wallabies. Without question, their success is fantastic, but how many people around the world outside of Australia and New Zealand are aware of the following names: Johnathan Thurston, Billy Slater, Cameron Smith, Greg Inglis, Darren Lockyer and, before this, Brad Fitler and Andrew Johns? To be honest, I could rattle off so many more names that all Australian pundits would agree consist of the best rugby athletes Australia has produced over the past thirty years. Yet, globally, it would only be the League supporters who would recognise the names.

For Rugby Union fans in South Africa, Japan, the British Isles, France and the rest of Europe and the globe, you may argue – who cares? To you – the avid followers of the fifteen-player version of the sport – your only concern is for what you see on the field. When your nation plays the Wallabies, you think you are playing the best. You care nothing for League. That thinking is fine; however, it does not take into account the fact that there is a superior opponent your nation has not yet defeated. And doesn't a true competitor enjoy testing themselves against the best?

Throughout all this, I should note that England – the home of both forms of the game – lose out. Their split has been divided along geographical and class lines. In the case of Rugby Union in England, they lose the abundant talent in the north to the English Super League or to the Australian National Rugby League. This loss of talent weakens the England Union national team's chances of success. With English Rugby League, they can never draw upon their best athletes to challenge Australia's domination over the League code. In the end, both sides lose out. Would South Africa have defeated England at the 2019 Rugby Union World Cup if England could draw upon all the talent of their nation? A definite yes may be argued by many, but since the question can be posed, it does cast doubt – even if only slightly.

The point is not to disrespect South Africa and their fans. South Africa are well-deserved Rugby Union World Champions. Of that there can be no doubt. However, are they the best rugby team on the planet? Before you respond, remember there are two forms of rugby – League and Union. I reiterate the point: South Africa never defeated the best rugby athletes and team Australia had to offer.

Therefore, the only sure way for any fan, player or administrator to determine which nation has the best rugby players

Chapter 4 – Why League and Union Should Merge

is for all the nations to play a united form of rugby, whereby the best athletes are not split along the lines of League or Union. And apart from one code completely wiping out the other – which has not happened since the split and is unlikely to happen any time soon – it would be an opportunity for the two sports to come together peacefully and implement a solution that would end the divide once and for all.

CHAPTER 5

Challenging Natural Prejudices

For there to be a change, there has to be a starting point. For any unification of the two rugby codes to take place, the first thing that must be tackled is prejudice. For any rugby follower in the traditional nations, there is a clear understanding of such prejudice. I will not use this process to repeat this point, other than to suggest that to hold such views is to be unaware of the truth. There are some things in life that are self-evident – the beauty and skill of rugby is such a truth. And since Union and League are variations of rugby, it is apparent that beauty and skill must be evident in both.

However, the fixed mindset is one that is hard to break down. For those who prefer Rugby Union and for those who enjoy Rugby League, I offer this notion – wouldn't it be great if all rugby fans united behind one game?

The proposal I present in this book basks in the sunlight of growth and opportunity and all I ask is one favour:

Please read to the very end before you make a judgement about the possibility of a unified code.

Chapter 5 – Challenging Natural Prejudices

If you are unable to overcome a set thought pattern of detestation against one code or the other and do not care for the concept of a single code, I ask that you read on for entertainment's sake. If you are open-minded and have a growth mindset than I consider that you are someone who seeks excellence and, if that's the case, I'll repeat yet again, please read to the very end before you make a judgement about the possibility of a unified code.

It is with this sole purpose and belief that only a single code – one that consists of elements from both games – that a solution for a single form of rugby can be achieved.

There will be factions with vested interests and supporters who are loyal to their code who would deny any chance of a unified version of the two games. They will highlight the many aspects of the two games that I have not covered. They will argue that in this abstract, no consideration was given to commercial representation. I do not challenge the commercial claims.

However, in order to address the commercial claim, I will pose the following questions:

Which TV station, news outlet, radio service, media format would not want to provide coverage for two of the best rugby teams in the world?

Which English or Australian rugby fan (of either code) would not be interested in witnessing the Kangaroos playing a combined England side at Twickenham?

I feel a merged code offers media a better product than the two separate sports can offer at present. I would argue that, under the current format, media partners are paying overs for a lesser product.

It is important to note that the premise of this brief is to highlight the similarities between the two codes and how a marriage between League and Union is not as difficult as one might have previously imagined.

SECTION TWO

The Rules of a United Rugby Game

CHAPTER 6

The Similarities Between the Two Codes

It cannot be denied that to the naked eye these two sports are eerily similar. At the same time, to the trained eye they are quite different. The differences shape the game and give the sporting contest a unique challenge. Still, the similarities are all too prevalent. There is more in common than not and so creating a single code is common sense.

The counter-argument to having a merged code is that it would then create a third tier of the sport. This argument is flawed but strangely accepted as being valid. The reason why it is flawed is that there are already different tiers of rugby. You have the fifteen-a-side version (Union), the thirteen-a-side version (League), Tens (Union variant), Nines (League variant), Sevens (Union and previously also League variants). On top of these contact versions, there are Tag, Touch, Wheelchair variations and the list goes on.

Yet, the argument persists. Hence, getting the balance in relation to the rules is fundamental to merging the fifteen and thirteen player variants of the rugby codes. Moreover, after addressing the club and international competition structures, the argument that a combined code creates a third type of rugby should be put to bed. To put it bluntly, the fans of Rugby League and Rugby Union will not abandon their code to follow a new type of rugby that cuts all traditional ties. The rugby fan will, however, follow their teams and nations into a single form of rugby, where their clubs, colours, histories and competitions are not lost but continue to thrive. Thus, establishing rules that can be accepted as fair and balanced is critical to any marriage between the codes.

Note: For some rules, I have provided a generalised summary while for others, I go into greater detail.

The Playing Field

The playing field may seem like a strange place to start, yet it is the easiest. The reason for this is that if people start arguing over the layout of the field, then the argument has deteriorated to a ridiculously low level.

In any case, the field layout should appease both sides of the rugby divide. The Rugby League 20-metre line would be replaced by the Rugby Union 22. The League 30-metre line would be removed, but instead of the 10-metre line for Union, the field markings would read 40 as is the case for League. Three markers would indicate where a 5-metre scrum may take place, but the 10-metre marker (close to the try line) as in League would remain the same. Obviously, the field markings become an essential factor when implementing kicking rules and have an impact on other rules – all of which will be revealed in the following pages.

The last point in terms of field markings is that the following image (see next page) offers the best compromise. Although as anyone who has played either form of rugby knows, when you are out on the field, the only field marking you care about is the try line.

Chapter 6 – The Similarities Between the Two Codes

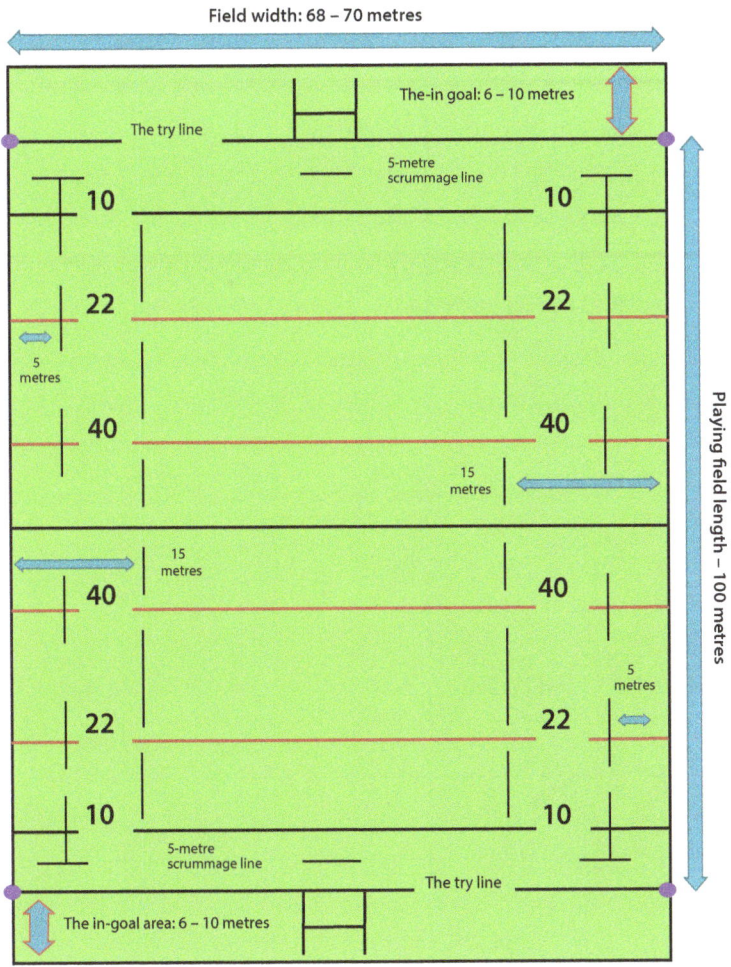

The Ball

Really? Yes, since diehards of the game will care about this point, the matter of the ball needs to be addressed. Generally speaking, you would allow the national competition to choose their preferred option. The National Rugby League uses the Steeden ball, whereas, Rugby Union uses the Gilbert ball.

The answer is simple: let the home nation choose the ball. However, in the case of international games when the sport is unified, the following points need to be taken into account:

- Let the competing companies present their case as to why their ball should be used.
- Get feedback from the players.
- Finally, choose the ball which provides a more fabulous spectacle for fans.

It is not an issue that needs to be determined straight away or be fixed for eternity. It could be a scenario whereby the company that produces the ball is rotated in accordance with a bidding process.

Put it this way – a passionate rugby player is unlikely to stop playing the game simply because the ball is branded differently.

Players Clothing

The matter of clothing worn by the players may seem so trivial; however, it is highlighted to reaffirm another similar aspect to the sport. The naysayers, doubters and those people with a fixed mindset might try to present any justification to shut down any discussion of why there should be a singular code of rugby. However, the uniform/dress code is not a valid reason.

Rugby Union and Rugby League have set requirements based around clothing apparel and set regulations. However, the regulations of mouthpieces, shoulder pads, headgear and studs on the players' boots share a collective value. The use of shin pads may no longer be a requirement in League; however, in Union where the scrum still has a prominent role, it is still a feature. Wearing hand mitts may be required in Europe during the winter months, but rarely (if ever) are they a requirement in Australia. Nevertheless, the two sports share a universal approach to endorsing a standard dress code.

Ultimately, it is a non-issue and, since both sports share the same beliefs regarding uniform, a combined approach should be adopted for any possible merger of the two games.

The Length of Matches

This is an important point to consider and, fortunately, this is where the two games align. In the case of both full-contact versions of rugby, the game is played over two halves of 40 minutes. This aspect must not change. The only real discernible difference between both codes is how the games end after each half. In Rugby League, once the siren blows, the game ends at the next completed tackle. For Rugby Union, it takes a game stoppage rather than a tackle to finish the match.

In a unified format, the Rugby Union style of ending the game would conclude the contest. This option would mean that the game stops when the play is concluded by a stoppage or penalty and not at the completion of the next tackle.

The suggested time allowance for a unified game of rugby is as follows:

- A full match – 80 minutes, consisting of two halves of 40 minutes each.
- Half-time break – 15 minutes.

Changes within the tournament and League mode and the governing bodies' response to extra time has an impact on how the period of extra time would be conducted. Some competitions use a set period while others go straight into a Golden Point scenario. However, the following template provides a suggested solution if extra time was required:

- Rest period after the game – 10 minutes

- Extra time – 20 minutes, consisting of two halves of 10 minutes each
- Extra time half-time break – 5 minutes.

Once again, some leagues and competitions may bypass the extra time situation in which case they would proceed to Golden Point. Furthermore, each jurisdiction may decide to implement a different style of Golden Point.

The following example provides one solution:

- Rest period after extra time – 5 minutes
- Golden Point – 20 minutes, consisting of two halves of 10 minutes each (game ends after first point scored)
- Golden Point half-time break – 5 minutes.

However, any set time for extra time and/or Golden Point can be determined by the local competition authority.

Naturally, both Rugby League and Rugby Union have rules and laws based around the length of matches, who keeps the time and what happens in case of injury. Logic suggests that the best process as deemed by the local governing body be implemented.

Since this response only addresses the full-contact versions of the sports, different time structures would be catered for in the case of the shorter versions of the game.

Knock-On and Forward Passes

Both of these are straightforward processes. For both forms of rugby, there is very little difference in the application of these rules. Nevertheless, on occasion, our eyes can deceive us when we as the spectator think a ball travels backwards but is ruled by the official to go forward. In reality, a forward pass is the same in Rugby League as it is in Rugby Union.

Chapter 6 – The Similarities Between the Two Codes

Moreover, a knock-on in Rugby League is the same as it is in Rugby Union.

There is no difference between the two codes. To spell it out for those who may be confused, a knock-on occurs when a player loses possession and control of the ball and it goes forward, either touching an opponent or the ground before the player regains possession. Meanwhile, a forward pass occurs when the player passes the ball and it travels the direction they are running and not backward as required by both games.

Q. What if it is a charge down? Is that still a knock-on?

No, of course not. Once again, there is no difference between the sports. Charging down a kick negates a knock-on and the game may continue.

Q. What if the ball is thrown backwards but hits the ground and bounces forward? Is that still a forward pass?

No. It is only a forward pass if the ball is thrown forward. If a deliberate forward pass is thrown, the defending team will receive a penalty kick.

Both League and Union apply the same rule in these two scenarios.

Q. What happens if a team throws a forward pass or knocks on and regathers? How does the game restart?

This aspect is where the slight difference comes into play. If the attacking team regains possession after committing the error (not an intentional forward pass), a handover will occur at the place of infringement and a Rugby League play-the-ball will ensue. If the ball travels into touch from the error, the play-the-ball is taken 15 metres infield.

Q. What! No scrum? What is your reasoning here?

The scrum does add another challenge for a possession; however, there are two issues to be considered here. First, the team that did not make a mistake receives no advantage. Second, the scrums in Rugby Union take so long to form, set and complete it halts the momentum of the game. This delay is where some people believe the two values of the sports differ. The game must make a compromise between maintaining integrity as a sport and being a 'product' for entertainment. A sport where the fans watch players reset for scrums adds nothing to the spectacle of the competition. Having the play-the-ball restart the game keeps the momentum of the contest rolling along, enhancing the enjoyment of fans.

Q. What happens if a team throws a forward pass or knocks on and then the defending team knocks on in an attempt to gain possession? How does the game restart then?

In this case, a scrum will ensue. The defending team failed to capitalise and, since they made an error as well, a challenge for possession will result. Though, as it currently stands, since they made the second error, they get the feed to the scrum. The scrum will occur at the place of infringement.

Q. What if there is a forward pass or knock-on in the in-goal area?

There are two scenarios in response to this question.

1. **The defending team:** If there is a knock-on or forward pass inside the in-goal upon attempted return of the ball, a Rugby League style goal-line dropout will result.
2. **The attacking team:** If it is the attacking team that knocks on or throws a forward pass in the in-goal

area when attempting to score, then a 22-metre tap kick may take place for the opposing team. A straightforward tap may occur or, if the team drop kicks the ball into touch from this restart, they will be awarded the lineout throw.

If an attacking player knocks on or throws forward the ball from the field of play and the ball goes into the opponents' in-goal and travels past the dead-ball line, the play restart will occur at the 22-metre line where a tap restart may ensue.

If the ball does not travel dead and the defending team has no advantage, a Rugby League play-the-ball will occur at the 5-metre line. From this position, the defending team will retreat 10-metres.

Q. What happens if a team throws a forward pass or knocks on deliberately?

Naturally, a forward pass that is deliberate can result in a penalty kick to the opposing team; however, from a deliberate knock-on, there is yet another difference between the two codes. In Rugby Union, this usually occurs when a player is attempting to stop the opposition from scoring. This action can result in a professional foul and the player being 'sin-binned'. On the other hand, in Rugby League a deliberate knockdown is only considered to be a knock-on. Under a single entity, as long as the player was onside, there is no professional foul. Under a unified model of rugby, the Rugby League aspect would be kept and, while some diehard Union fans will probably lament the rule, I suggest the following:

It's a major tournament, and the opposition is pressing your line. They throw a pass. You stick your hand out. If the ball sticks, you can run downfield and turn momentum. If it does not stick and falls to the ground, you could be 'sin-binned' for a professional foul.

If you do not think that this punishment for the opportunistic action is harsh, then so be it. Understandably, maybe that is not how Rugby Union's rule was designed or intended to be applied, but it has been used in this manner previously (rightly or wrongly). Rugby League's method of addressing this action is cleaner.

Q. You mentioned in this section, Rugby League play-the-balls, lineouts and scrums.

Yes, I did. I will cover these in more detail soon.

Onside and Offside

Apart from the breakdown of the ruck and the numbers of players on the field, the defending position is one of the most discernible differences between League and Union. In League, it is 10 metres from the ball, whereas in Union, a player only needs to retreat behind the last feet. The challenge for this aspect of the game is how to allow for a free-flowing contest. Players in the modern game are extremely fit and so a game tailored to defence can become a little boring. For this reason, with the tackling and ruck system applied and with a sense of compromise, I have recommended the 5-metre retreat. Ultimately, the onside and offside rule is almost identical in both codes; however, the following details provide further clarity.

Some basic guidelines for the retreating defence include:
- Retreat 5 metres in general play from a tackle (except the two markers).
- Retreat 10 metres from the back of the scrum.
- Retreat 10 metres from the lineout.
- Retreat 10 metres from a penalty.
- Retreat 10 metres from a kick-off or line dropout.

Chapter 6 – The Similarities Between the Two Codes

- Retreat 10 metres in a changeover of a set of six.

It is important to note the only real difference between the two sports revolves around loitering in the ruck where in the case of League, punishment results more often than not in a penalty. An attacking player in front of the ruck at the cycle of play is instantly regarded as offside. That particular player can only be considered onside by retreating behind the ruck. However, if while offside this player infringes on the defence, a penalty to the defending team will be awarded. This element is very similar to the rules associated with the ruck in Rugby League, but not too dissimilar to Union that it could be an issue.

On the other hand, in the case of the defence, they are considered to be offside the moment they have not retreated the set distance required for that particular element of the game. Any defensive offside penalty allows the other team either a kick for touch, a kick for a goal or when the referee is satisfied that the defence has had ample time to retreat the penalty distance, a tap may be taken. This interpretation of the rule applies in the general field of play, but when the play moves to the in-goal area, offside is waivered. Any breach of the rule here will result in a goal-line dropout.

Q. What about accidental offside?

In conjunction with the forward pass and knock-on, an accidental offside will result in a handover, and the Rugby League play-the-ball will ensue. The defending team must then retreat 10 metres.

Q. What about offside from kicks in play?

For matters relating to kicking and being offside, the rules of both codes apply. The offside player must not impede or advance within the 10-metre area of the ball. Only once that 10-metre zone has been breached is the player onside again. There may be slight variations in the offside rule when it comes to kicking (due to Union's preference for the kicking form). Nevertheless, the fact remains that these differences are so minute that they do not constitute a valid reason for not having a unified form of rugby.

CHAPTER 7

The Differences Between the Two Codes

Yes, it is an undeniable truth – the two rugby codes of League and Union are two separate sports. Despite sharing the same roots and heritage, the two games have drifted further apart over time. Almost from the outset, Rugby League was designed to please the spectators – the paying public – and the results were evident early on. They reduced the numbers of players from 15 to 13 and scrapped lineouts. They also stopped contesting scrums at each ruck and established the play-the-ball feature. These three fundamental differences have set the two games apart. In reality, Rugby League has always been willing to change their rules to make their game more appealing to the fans. On the other hand, Rugby Union progressed with limited changes until the game turned professional in 1995. Since this time, the game has sought ways to engage fans better and maintain its popularity around the world.

However, despite everything that is similar between the two forms of rugby, it is addressing the variations that will be the decisive factor in appeasing the fans and creating a single code. It should be noted that any change to the differences between the codes may cause heated argument, but compromise is achievable.

The variations: the point system, kicking, lineouts, scrums, tackles, play-the-ball/ruck and, finally, player numbers.

Scoring

At present, there is not much difference in scoring between the two codes. This element of the game should not be one that is hard to compromise, yet, no doubt it will raise issues. The central component that needs to be addressed is how much value to place on different aspects of the game. In Rugby League, the try is valued more than the ability to punish a team with a penalty or dropkicks. Whereas, in Union (and this is more so the case in the northern hemisphere) there is a focus on the ability to kick penalty goals or take dropkicks.

The easy solution would be to allow local and national competitions to allocate their scoring system; however, this negates the need for international conformity.

The ideal point scoring system is Rugby League's point system which includes:

A try / penalty try = 4 points

A penalty goal / conversion = 2 points

Drop / field goal = 1 point

Addressing Bias

As I have previously stated, Rugby League was, and remains, my preferred rugby code. However, that is not why I have proposed the League form of scoring. It simply offers more balance in scoring. In Union, two penalty goals and the team who has scored no tries could be ahead of a team that has scored a single unconverted try. In League, they would be tied. Also, I feel it an injustice that a team can kick two drop goals and be ahead of a team that has scored an unconverted try. I recognise the fact that 'going for the try' is, without doubt, a part of the fabric of playing and supporting rugby in Australia. The favoured idea held 'down under' is that 'going for the try' is the be-all and end-all. The notion that being defeated by an opposition that scored fewer tries but can kick the ball 40 metres out from the try line leaves a nasty taste in the mouth – not only for the players but for the fans as well.

To the hardcore Rugby Union fan, I offer this sage wisdom – there was a time when tries in Union were worth 4 points. They only increased to 5 points in the 1990s. Penalty kicks have not always been 3 points either. The point system for both codes has changed over time and no doubt will be modified sometime in the future. Importantly, no-one has stopped watching their preferred rugby code because of a point system change.

To conclude the discussion of match points: if the proposal for an Australian Kangaroos versus the best of English League and Union players match was offered and to be played at Twickenham, would you care if the try was worth five or four points?

Kicking

Kicking is such a fundamental part of the game; more so in Rugby Union than in Rugby League, but essential nonetheless. As a consequence, I have aimed to cover all aspects of kicking that occur in gameplay.

In terms of kicking, the following applications should, for the most part, cover any concerns readers may have. I am aware that I'm not able to review every aspect in great detail. To obtain all the desired detail, one would have to explore the pages of Rugby League's and Rugby Union's rulebooks in-depth. However, fundamentally, I've attempted to present an accurate reflection of the commonalities between the two sports. Dismissing the concept of a single rugby code as a possibility due to a minor lack of detail is akin to not buying the almost perfect house because you do not like the curtains. Remember, if the standard rule book were to be applied, the best elements of the kicking laws should be (and within reason would be) included in any merged entity.

Kicking is an aspect that defines both sports. Both codes incorporate it into their game, yet their manner alters all the same. I hope the following detail as many scenarios as possible.

The Kick-off

The dropkick of Union would be applied to a merged game. I recommend adapting the Rugby Union model and mixing it with elements of Rugby League. In League, a place kick from a kicking tee is the usual norm while in Union, a dropkick takes place. I have chosen the Union method since it allows no-one else aside from the players and officials to be on the field. In League games, often you see the trainer remain on the ground in back play. The notion that a trainer needs to be on the field is ridiculous and only acts as interference in play.

The elements of League that have been included is if the ball travels dead in-goal. The receiving team then has to return with a goal-line dropout. Moreover, if the ball is kicked out anywhere on the full, the referee would award a penalty at the halfway line, allowing for a far more significant advantage to the receiving team. Naturally, the ball must travel 10 metres, with failure to do so resulting in another penalty. However, if the ball does reach the sideline and bounces (after hitting the ground) and leaves the field of play, the kicking team will be awarded the lineout throw.

Lastly, there are no 'marks' from a kick-off. The ball is in play the moment it leaves the boot until the next break in play – however long that may be.

The Conversion

In Rugby Union, after a try is scored the defending team can attempt to charge down the kick (as long as they have retreated behind their goal line). This feature is an exciting element of the game and, therefore, it would be retained. Moreover, issues around the penalty try or League's 8-point try can be kept. Issues such as holding the ball in windy conditions and other aspects of the conversion are almost identical for both sports. So the conversion guidelines of both games will remain the same.

The Penalty Kick

Once again, both sports are almost identical on this point. The defending team will need to retreat the 10 metres and they will not be able to distract the kicker. Failure to do so gives the kicking team the potential to receive another penalty. The only difference is that if after a penalty attempt (not from a penalty try) the kicked ball 'goes dead', then the opposing team must return the ball to play via a 22-metre line dropout.

40 – 22 / 22 – 40

The 40 – 22 / 22 – 40 rule is a modification of Rugby League's 40 – 20 rule. However, players and fans from nations where Rugby Union is prominent may think it is Rugby Union's 50 – 22 rule. In a way it is but that rule was originally taken and then adapted from Rugby League. There is no reason for anybody to complain about the implementation of the 40 – 22 law.

In League, the team that kicks a 40 – 20 receives a tap restart. In any unified system, it would only mean that if your team was successful in a 40 – 22 kick, you would win the lineout throw.

Ball into Touch

A ball in general play (not a penalty kick, dropout or kick-off) cannot be kicked into touch on the full. This is regardless of if the ruck is behind the 22-metre line as is currently the case in Union. If a kicked ball goes into touch on the full, the ball is brought back to the placement of the kick and a handover with a Rugby League play-the-ball will happen. The defending team (the team that kicked out on the full resulting in turnover) will then retreat 10 metres in preparation for the next play.

The Goal-line Dropout / 22 Dropout

This law is adopted straight from Rugby League. Why? Because it works. If the defending team knocks the ball dead, then a goal-line dropout will result. If a defending team throw a forward pass, knock on or ground the ball in-goal, a goal-line dropout results.

A 22 dropout occurs if a penalty kick misses and goes dead. Then the defending team can dropkick from the 22-metre line.

All kicking rules that apply to the kick-off also apply to these dropouts.

The Mark

The 'mark' only occurs when the ball is caught from a kick on the full in the team's in-goal area. If a 'mark' is taken, then the ball is returned to the 22-metre line for a quick tap restart.

From this restart, the defending team would need to retreat 10 metres.

The team conducting the tap restart can (if they choose to do so), dropkick the ball into touch where they may seek to gain positional advantage and a lineout throw.

Obviously, challenging for the ball (from a kick) in League is prevalent, especially when an attacking kick is placed. All rules around player safety apply – that is no tackling players in the air or knocking them without attempting to take a fair catch.

To recap this section on kicking – as previously stated, not every detail has been covered. However, the two codes have laws that demonstrate how the set rules listed above are implemented.

Lineouts

Rugby Union uses lineouts whereas Rugby League got rid of them in their formative years as a sport. Under a unified code, they will be maintained. Any ball that travels legally into touch that is through a general play kick, legal pass, fumble or penalty kick will result in a lineout.

Moreover, the laws (the majority) of the lineout that Rugby Union present will be maintained. Albeit, no maul can develop from the lineout. This matter will be addressed later in the tackle section of this book. If a maul does present to form, the referee will call, 'Held', and the play progression will cease. At this point, the player with the ball must go to ground or play-the-ball; if the play proceeds in a forward motion, an obstruction penalty will be awarded to the defending team.

Some Rugby League fans may lament the inclusion of the lineout due to its slowness of delivery. Yet, this complaint is unwarranted. The benefits of the lineout far outweigh any negative aspects. It is undeniable that a lineout adds another element of contest into a very physical sport, which can only be considered as beneficial to a single rugby code.

In terms of the number of players in the lineout – that would depend on the number of players the unified code chooses to have on the field. For more information about this aspect of the game … read on.

Scrums

Common Belief: *Rugby Union scrums are serious matters but Rugby League scrums are a joke.*

That belief is common among rugby fans around the world. In many regards, it is hard to argue with this viewpoint. In League, the hooker usually lines up at the lock position and the props no longer bind. There is no real push and the ball is fed nowhere near the centre of the scrum. Also, it's not always done by the halfback. So why have them, right? League purist still argue that they are a restart where the defensive line numbers are reduced. This point holds some weight as some tries are scored from set scrum plays; however, for the most part, a scrum in League is a waste of time.

Conversely, Rugby Union scrums remain an art form. They are a battle of strength and superiority. They are contested … to a point. Arguments can be made against Union scrums as well. They take so long to set and often collapse. After multiple attempts to get it right, a penalty is awarded.

Meanwhile, the fans at home are grabbing their remotes, trying to see what other shows are available on the 'idiot box'. Then, if a scrum is performed correctly, it is becoming increasingly rare for the opposition to win against the feed.

Chapter 7 – The Differences Between the Two Codes

Union fans will disagree, but the scrum in Union, while still more relevant, is becoming a predictable event.

I do not mean to be blasé about the scrum. When done correctly, it is everything it is designed to be. It is just that in both codes, it is no longer representative of its original purpose.

Nevertheless, in a unified system, scrums would be maintained, though with much less focus than is currently the case in Rugby Union. The reasons for this are varied and are outlined below.

League no longer has contested scrums. A hooker in League is very different from a hooker in Union. In League, the position goes by the nickname, 'Dummy Half', which references its ball-playing attributes, while in Union a hooker makes up the front row. It would not be possible to merge the two codes and straightaway implement contested scrums – the dangers are far too apparent.

Q. So how will scrums be included within a unified code?

Initially, and until such time that recruitment could match the progress of the squads, uncontested scrums would occur. This slight adjustment to contested scrums may take some time but it removes the risk of serious injury. Once all teams have adjusted and have players who are capable of performing the duties required in a scrum, contested scrums will continue to form a central part of the game. Once contested scrums are in play again, the safety measures applied by the current Union laws could be implemented.

Q. What do you mean, 'much less focus on the scrum'?

Exactly that. The only time a scrum will occur in the modified version of the game will be when there is a double knock-on or when one team throws a forward pass and the opposition fumbles when trying to gain possession. In Rugby Union, a team may select a scrum restart in place of a penalty. However, if there are any penalties in the modified version, a League tap or penalty kick (either for touch or goal) will be the options that can be selected. Therefore, under a merged version, scrums will occur in limited form. They can be contested (when safe to do so), but they will have far less relevance in the modern game.

Q. Are you for real? The scrum is a fundamental part of the game.

Yes, I am serious. The scrum's future is limited. Think about it logically: there is all this weight, tightened and compacted and then bound, which bangs into another set of bodies holding roughly the same weight mass. That is a recipe for disaster. It may work among elite players, but filter that practice down through the ranks and it only becomes a health hazard. For this reason, the scrum is on the endangered list for both codes.

Q. Are there penalties from scrum infringements?

Yes, but like League, they become a differential penalty. So, no kick at goal can be taken, only a tap restart or a kick for touch.

Q. How many players form the scrum?

I am not going to answer this question yet. You will need to read on to discover the answer.

So to recap this section on scrums – the scrum stays, but in a much more reduced role. And when it is safe to do so, it will be contested.

Chapter 7 – The Differences Between the Two Codes

The Tackle and Ruck

To state the obvious: The tackle and ruck styles are a fundamental difference between the two codes. Except for the numbers of players on the field, the ruck remains the most significant difference between the two sports. How a player is tackled and plays the ball and the nature of limited and an unlimited tackle count has an impact on the skills required in the ruck.

As a consequence, how the attacking player approaches being tackled also changes. In Rugby League, a player attempts to break through the line rather than seek a quick entry to the ground as in Union. Therefore, this motion alters the nature of the tackle. In League, the defensive player aims to wrap the ball to stop an offload and then commits to a tackle. On the other hand, in Union, the aim is to chop a player down and to rotate him so he can no longer feed the ball back towards his team.

Moreover, in League, after a tackle is completed, a play-the-ball ensues and the attacking team has limited tackles in order to make the most impact. In Rugby Union, a ruck occurs and the team keeps the ball for as long as they maintain possession.

This variation may be a sticking point for the two codes. Thereby, in my proposal, I have opted for the limited tackle rule applied by League, but with Union's ruck style. Yes, there have been slight alterations; however, if a single rugby was to exist, compromise would be a requirement.

Q. So, please explain. How can a Union ruck be used, but with a limited tackle count?

When the ball carrier is tackled to the ground as is the case in Union, he will then place the ball backwards. This act will be considered a tackle. An attacking team will have a limited amount of tackles to use the ball.

Q. How many tackles does an attacking team get?

At the outset, the League form will be used. This encompasses six tackles – unless the ball is touched and they get a repeat set or if the defending team regathers from a knock-on, in which case the first tackle is a zero tackle. Also, when a team restarts play from a 22-metre tap, the first tackle is a zero tackle which results in a 7-tackle set.

Q. What if a tackler gets held upright in a standing position?

In Union, this would cause a stoppage. However, in a merged code, the referee will call 'Held' and the player would be required to play-the-ball League style.

Q. What? Do you have two types of ruck manoeuvres?

Yes, the aim is to keep the game flowing. If a player can get to the ground, he does not need to get to his feet to play the ball. Instead, he can just place it behind himself. If he doesn't get to the ground, the League form can be used. Nevertheless, it is advantageous for the attacking team to keep the defence on retreat so getting to the ground will be crucial for any quick play to occur.

Q. Can defending teams make a play for the ball?

In Rugby Union, every tackle is a challenge for possession. That is the main reason why the ball runner tries to get to the ground. The attacking player does not want to lose possession of the ball. In League, the ball can only be stolen one-on-one. Consequently, the answer to the question is 'yes'. The defending team can make a play for the ball; however, it is a slight adjustment. When the ball carrier goes to ground, only those players involved in the tackle, who maintain their feet and are in a 'marker' position can play the ball.

If the player maintains their feet and does not go to ground, then only a one-on-one steal can occur.

Q. Marker position – what do you mean?

In Rugby League, the defending team has two markers when a tackle is completed. This process could be applied in a unified code. These players – if they formed part of the tackle and have maintained their feet – can reach down into the ruck to challenge for possession. However, if the attacking team have a player who comes in to protect the ruck, then a challenge for possession can no longer take place and play continues. Only two markers are allowed. All other players must retreat five metres (from the position of the ruck). This interpretation is a slight variation of League and Union rules. In League, the defending team retreats ten metres. In Union, the defending team retreats to the last feet situated at the ruck.

Q. So the markers can challenge for the ball?

Yes, as long as these players were involved in the tackle and are standing square. Standing square requires the defender to stand directly opposite from the tackled player and not to come in and attack the ball from the side. No other players other than the tacklers can make a play for the ball.

Q. What about the defensive line? Where do they stand?

As stated in the onside/offside section, the defending team from a tackle will retreat five metres. If either the player gets to ground or not, all defenders (except the two markers) will retreat five metres.

Q. Can a maul develop?

No, once the attacking team relies on assistance to push the ball forward, the referee will call 'Held' and a play-the-ball will need to be taken. If forward progression continues, the referee may award a penalty to the defending team citing obstruction. The only time assistance can be offered to the ball runner is if they are being pushed back in goal or in to touch.

Q. What happens if the attacking team is caught in possession after a set of tackles?

The same process as in League: a turnover will result. In which case, a Rugby League play-the-ball will occur and the defending team on a handover in possession will retreat 10 metres.

Q. What happens if a defender does not release the tackled player?

If the player gets to ground or not, once the referee calls 'Tackled' or 'Held', the defenders must release the tackled player. If not, the tackle count may be reset (as in League) or a penalty will result. The attacking team then can choose either a quick tap, a kick for touch or a penalty kick.

Q. What about the tackled player? What responsibilities do they hold?

Firstly, for a tackled player standing or going to ground, the ball must always be played backwards towards their goal line. A forward play will result in a knock-on ruling. A handover will take place as a consequence.

If a player goes to ground, they must not keep hold of the ball. They must place it back immediately. If they hold the

Chapter 7 – The Differences Between the Two Codes

ball, as is the case in Union, a penalty will be awarded to the defending team.

If the attacking player remains standing, they must play the ball backwards as is the case in Rugby League. If they play the football forward, the referee will indicate a knock-on. If they baulk at playing the ball, the referee may allow the defence to creep forward.

Ultimately, a player with the ball must immediately do one of the following:
- If not tackled, get up with the ball and either run, pass or kick it.
- If tackled to the ground, release the ball backwards.
- If tackled but not to the ground, play the football backwards.

Failure to do so will result in a penalty or handover (depending on the offence) being awarded to the defending team.

Q. What if, during the tackle, the ball becomes unplayable?

If the ball is unplayable because a player has fallen over the ruck either by accident or to slow play, a penalty will ensue. The ruck must be cleared as quickly as possible and the referee will make a judgement call based on that interpretation.

Fundamentally, the tackled player must release or play the ball as quickly as possible.

Q. Can the attacking team stop the defending team for challenging for the ball?

Yes, if a player is tackled to the ground, a teammate who is without the ball can stand over or near the ball to prevent any of the opponents getting possession of it. However, they must not lie on the ball. Standing over the ball negates the defensive team's right to challenge for the ball. This player will be acting as a blocker. The blocker must always maintain their feet. Once the blocker is in place, the markers can no longer attack for the ball.

Q. What if a teammate who is without the ball does not maintain feet or lies on the ball?

If a teammate of the tackled player accidentally falls on the ball, they must move as quickly as possible to clear the ruck. If a blocker fails to maintain their feet and they hinder the marker's ability to challenge for the ball, the defending team will be awarded a penalty.

If an attacking player does not go to ground in a tackle, there is no need for a blocker and a Rugby League style play-the-ball will occur.

Q. What happens if a player's momentum takes them into the in-goal?

If a tackled player's momentum carries the ball runner into the in-goal, the player can score a try. If they get held up and it is not the last tackle, the ball is taken back to the 5-metre line. If it was the last tackle, a handover would result and the defending team will play the ball 10 metres out from their try line.

Q. Can a tackled player reach out for a try if tackled?

No, the ball must always be placed backwards. If a player is tackled near the goal line, that player is not allowed to reach out and ground the ball on or over the goal line to score a try. This act is considered a double movement and is a Rugby League rule.

If the tackle was not complete – that is when the player goes to ground and no hands remained attached – the tackle

Chapter 7 – The Differences Between the Two Codes

may be considered incomplete and, consequently, the attacking player may make a forward move for the try line.

Q. When can play continue after a tackle?

The defending team can move forward once the referee has indicated that the ball has been cleared. The ball is cleared when it is free to be picked up at the ruck by the attacking team.

Q. How should the game end?

In League, the game finishes after the completed tackle. In Union, the game continues until there is a stoppage. The Union-ending version should be applied to a merged game. In this way, the game will only end by the ball going out of the field of play.

Q. Can a team be allowed more than six tackles?

Yes, League rules apply here. If the ball is touched by the defending team but the attacking team regain possession, a six again will be indicated by the referee. If a ruck infringement occurs, the referee has the option to blow a penalty or rule six again. A seven-tackle set happens when there is a turnover from a knock-on or when the ball goes dead in-goal and a 22-metre tap is taken.

Q. So, a quick summary, please. Describe the tackle/ruck in the modified game.

The ball runner runs forward and gets tackled to the ground. Once they hit the ground, they must place the ball back towards their try line (as is the case in Union). Now the tacklers may regain their feet, stand square and challenge for the ball. If another defending player not involved in the tackle stands at 'marker', they cannot challenge for the ball. The attacking team can also negate any challenge for the ball by having a blocker stand over the ruck. As long as the blocker stands over the ruck, the defensive team cannot challenge for the ball. A defending team (apart from two markers) will retreat five metres from the ruck. Once the ball is cleared, the play can continue. The attacking team will be allowed a set of six tackles to progress the ball as far downfield as possible.

The other scenario for a tackle is if the ball runner does not go to ground and is held standing by the defence. Then, once the referee gives the tackled call, a tackle is completed. The play-the-ball will result (League style). A defending team (apart from two markers) will retreat five metres from the ruck. Once the ball can be picked up by the attacking team, the ball is clear for play. The attacking team will be allowed a set of six tackles to progress the ball as far downfield as possible.

Playing Numbers

This positional alignment, along with the ruck interpretation, is a fundamental difference between the two codes.

Q. How many players are there on the field?

The reasonable compromise is 14 players. This number reduces the forwards by two, but adds a rover type position. My preference is 13 players, but that is my bias. Before the rage emerges from your soul, I will explain the reasoning.

The main reason why I feel that 13 players are preferable to 15 is simply to open up space on the field in order to allow a more attacking style of rugby to take place. This decision is not intended to be an insult to Rugby Union supporters; however, with two fewer players per team on the field, there

Chapter 7 – The Differences Between the Two Codes

would be more space to break the line and more room to score tries. For the most part, the aim of Rugby League's forefathers for a fast, free-flowing game has been accomplished.

World Rugby failed to reduce the number of players to 13 due to the desire to maintain its traditions, but also (and probably more importantly) because this alteration would mean that it was too similar to Rugby League. However, a merger between League and Union may be the circuit breaker needed to achieve such a change.

Nevertheless, it is recognised that many supporters of Rugby Union would savage a suggestion of reducing the player numbers from 15 to 14 or 13 … and the same scenario in reverse for Rugby League. Any notion of increasing the players on the field to 14 or 15 players would result in a brutal response.

It is for these reasons that determining the number of players allowed on the pitch is critical if ever a merger of the two codes were to occur.

Q. How would the sports determine if there were 15, 14 or 13 players on the field?

Once again, without doubt prejudice will rear its ugly head on this matter. These two sports with their long and proud traditions would struggle to let go and adapt. The two sports could both compromise and reach an agreement of 14 players; however, that tactic would still be met with some resistance. Hence, in a free world, the only way to progress would be to hold a vote. Also, another way of finding the perfect solution could be to implement a trial and error approach.

Q. What is the trial and error method?

Easy – professional clubs (League Vs Union) compete against each other in a series of matches played under the compromised rules (as outlined in this book). Some games would have 13 or 14 players and others 15. This trial may help the playing group, the clubs and the fans to decide which style they prefer. Naturally, the trial would be undertaken before any vote took place. It also allows for the players to offer their opinions on what they think worked and what did not.

Q. A vote? Who votes – the governing bodies of each country?

No, in terms of votes, it would be the clubs and their players. With reference to the combined English competition which is described later in this book, every professional club would vote on which system they preferred – 13, 14 or 15 players. Again, especially for England, the vote needs to be fair and equitable.

Ideally, each club would get a playing group vote and use this to determine the club's vote of preference.

Q. That's a vote in England. What about the rest of the world?

With regards to the Australian and New Zealand based rugby competition (NRL), each club would have a vote on their preference. Once again, seeking feedback from the playing group would be crucial.

For competitions in France and the Pro 14, they would conduct a trial as well and then proceed to vote.

Q. Again, what about the rest of the world?

In all fairness, if the major rugby nations of Australia, England, France and New Zealand were to adopt a modified game, then they could act as negotiators for other nations to transition the two forms into a single sport.

Of course, you could expect that difficulties will arise as a result of this process due to the fact that Rugby League

Chapter 7 – The Differences Between the Two Codes

is not as dominant globally. No doubt, this obstacle would be a concern for League supporters. Nevertheless, if the NRL incorporated the New Zealand Super Rugby Clubs and the New Zealand Rugby Union into the Australasian Competition and England competed as one, then that unity may be enough to present a new path forward. Once again, would any country be happy to continue playing only by Union rules if New Zealand, Australia, England and France adopted the single form proposed in this book?

Q. What if the votes fail to determine 13, 14 or 15 players?

Then we will stay with the status quo we have had for more than one hundred years and two forms of rugby would remain. A fractured game would stand, and the two sports of Rugby League and Rugby Union would continue to compete against each other and challenge each other for players, administrators, sponsors and fans. The argument as to which is the best rugby team in the world would never be answered.

Q. What about the amateur game?

A merged code in the professional ranks does not necessarily mean an immediate merged code in amateur form. Therefore, the 15-a-side version and the 13-a-side version may adjust slowly over time so that eventually, after a phasing in period, the amateur forms become more aligned to the professional style of the game.

To explain this point in more detail: in Australia, the professional game implemented the 10-metre rule and following this adjustment, country rugby league in Australia followed suit. Furthermore, in England, when the sport of Rugby League switched over to summer, the amateur game took some time and consulted with its members, the sports' governing body, the players and clubs. It was a fair process, and eventually, the amateur clubs moved to play their games in the summer.

It is not without reason to expect the same to occur under a merged form of the game, especially when the rules are so much alike. Nothing should be forced and, therefore, if a vote (with equal representation) were held about the playing numbers, then complaints would be kept to a minimum.

Q. Isn't the fact that there is a 13-a-side version and a 15-a-side version of rugby an indication that players and clubs have taken a vote already?

I understand that reasoning but it is a misrepresentation of history. The game is split according to geographical, cultural and historical criteria rather than any on-field rule mechanism. By this, I mean the Northern Union and the New South Wales Rugby League (League) only began to be able to compensate players. The differing rules are a consequence of the split. The game of League only disposed of the lineout and the two extra players for commercial reasons. In League's history, the sport changed to 13 players for purposes of entertainment. The rationale was that fewer players open up the field of play and this allows for a more exciting contest to occur. This change, in turn, could draw more spectators through the gates thereby making an increased profit for clubs so that they were more financially viable.

Over a century later, the numbers of players on the field has become a badge of honour for each sport. Each fan might think of playing numbers in the following manner:

To League fans, increasing the numbers on the field would be a backward step in the evolution of the sport.

To Union fans, decreasing the numbers on the field would be an insult to the memory and history of the sport.

Chapter 7 – The Differences Between the Two Codes

A neutral approach with no bias towards either side would present a compromise – that of 14 players where it implements a system requiring one less forward, by the creation of a rover position that can fill any backline gap.

These points are valid and hold weight. And since they hold weight, the number of players on the field presents the greatest obstacle in forming a single code of rugby. Consequently, I go back to a point I raised earlier – let a vote by the players and the clubs decide the future of the two sports.

Q. Okay, so we have a merged game – how many bench players?

If there were to be a merger between League and Union, regardless of if there were 13, 14 or 15 players, there would be a range of five to seven bench players (depending on the number of players on the field). Nevertheless, there would be only seven substitution allowances.

Q. How does the substitution of players work?

A team can use a maximum of seven substitutions. There may be cases where a Head Injury Assessment or a blood bin is required, in which case, all the rules and regulations under the laws currently employed by both codes would be completed.

Q. What about acts of foul play?

Currently, Rugby League and Rugby Union share rules with regards to send-offs and 'sin bins' and, consequently, these would be maintained. Naturally, there are slight variations in interpretations of playing laws; however, a new code would err on the side of caution and take the most conservative approach.

Q. So one last time, how many players would be on the field for any one team?

There are three options: League's 13 players, a compromise of 14 or Union's 15 players.

Let the trials begin and let the players and clubs decide.

CHAPTER 8

The Officials

I write this statement with all due respect – could you imagine a game against the Australian Kangaroos and the South African Springboks not taking place because people were unhappy with the way the referee pointed his whistle for a try?

I understand that the officials of the game, despite being a required element, are often overlooked. The delay mentioning them is not intended to be an insult. To be succinct, the match officials' role and responsibilities change very little between the two codes.

Checking playing attire and equipment would continue and their duties in implementing the laws of the unified version of the game (including lineouts, tackle, rucks, and scrums) would remain their responsibility. The officials control the game on the pitch.

Referees and Match Officials

For some time, Rugby League within the National Rugby League implemented a two-referee system. Upon the restart of the fractured season of 2020, they resorted to a single-referee system. Naturally, the use and rules of the referees and match officials can be determined by the local competition governing body. Yet, for the sake of international conformity, set standard guidelines would be applied.

Clearly, any debate about this could take place further into the development of a single form of rugby. Notwithstanding, the following information presents an option that could be applied.

In all games, the match officials will consist of the following:

1. A referee
2. Two sideline officials also referred to as touch judges
3. A match official who is also referred to as the video referee
4. Time-keeper.

It is possible in some competitions for in-goal judges or an extra referee to be chosen; however, that would be a decision for the governing body of the local competition.

Nothing about their role would change. The referee is the ultimate authority on the field.

The referee may:

- Consult or ignore the advice of other officials.
- Change their mind on a ruling if they are updated about the issue from an assisting official.
- Take time to explain their verdict to the two designated captains of the teams participating in the match.
- At his/her discretion, temporarily suspend or prematurely terminate a match because of adverse weather, undue interference by spectators, misbehaviour by

players, or any other cause which, in his/her opinion, interferes with his/her control of the game.
- Dismiss players and trainers from the field.
- Determine who is allowed or not allowed on the field of play.

The only exception to that last two points is for trainers who seek to attend an injured player; however, they would inform the sideline official upon their entry. If a trainer was on the field for any other purpose, the referee might remove them from the ground.

Naturally, the importance of respecting match officials is paramount and, thus, any harassment of officials would be dealt with harshly. Rugby League and Rugby Union are tough sports. They should not fall into a style where referees are confronted by players and are disrespected as is exemplified in other sporting codes around the world.

Importantly: Nothing about the roles of the referees should change. The referee is the ultimate authority on the field and they implement the laws of the game.

Match Official Signals

When the referee is required to give a decision relating to the game, whenever possible, he or she shall indicate the nature of his or her choice by making the appropriate signal. This idea should not be a contentious issue. What's more, if it is decided that the governing bodies for different club competitions may choose different signals, this should not be a deterrent to unifying the codes.

The following information has been taken from both Union and League. Note, not every aspect of the rulebook has been covered, but it is designed to act as a guide so that the process can be completed.

Referee Signals	
Matter under consideration	**Signal to be applied – League or Union**
Try and penalty try	League
Penalty	League
Penalty for backchat	League
Forming a scrum	Union
Scrum advantage	Union
Handling ball in the scrum	Union
Incorrect feed of scrum	Union
Failing to bind	Union
Prop pulling on opponent in scrum	Union
Prop pulling down opponent in scrum	Union
Intentionally diving to the ground	Union
Wheeling scrum	Union
Foot up by prop	Union
Time – Off	Union
Offside – Penalty given	League
High tackle	Union
Advantage	Union
Knock-on	Union
Punching penalty	Union
Lineout throw	Union
Offside at lineout	League signal for offside to be used
Throw in at lineout not straight	Union
Closing the gap in lineout	Union
Barging in lineout	Union
Leaning on player in lineout	Union

Chapter 8 – The Officials

Pushing opponent in lineout	Union
Early lifting in lineout	Union
Sin bin	Both optional
Send off	Both optional
Time stopped	League
Blood injury	Union
Head injury	Both optional
Video referee	Both optional
Held up in goal	League
Kick at goal successful / unsuccessful	Same
Penalty kick	League
Dropout	League
Play on	League
Six again	League
Ball touch in flight	League
Held	League
Failure to release tackled player	League
Headbutt	League
Illegal steal of ball	League
Illegal dragging of player after tackle	League
Last tackle	League
Tackled on the last	League

Touch Judges / Sideline Official Signals	
Matter under Consideration	Signal to be Applied – League or Union
Try and penalty try	League
Player in touch	Same
Ball in touch	Same
Kick / penalty kick	Same
Ball dead in-goal	League
Lineout	Union

Interpretations

This should be a more straightforward process. For both forms of rugby, there is very little difference in the application of these rules and it only becomes a matter of interpretation of the laws. This issue is already frustrating for fans, especially in Rugby Union, where different nations focus on various aspects of the laws.

Prejudice

The supporters of the Union form of rugby would dismiss the notion that League implements any deterrents to some matters – especially regarding foul play. This belief system has little or no factual basis. Yet, at this point, we shouldn't get drawn into a League vs Union battle but, rather, aim to find common ground.

In any case, when you consider the two sports, some elements are either identical or remarkably similar. Therefore, logically speaking, compromise is easy to achieve.

Chapter 8 – The Officials

Q. Both sports apply advantage differently – how would that work?

Ultimately, it is the referee who indicates an advantage when an infringement from the opposing team disrupts the flow of the game. If no advantage is gained, the referee can always decide to issue a penalty.

Q. What happens if the referee accidentally interferes with play?

A Rugby League style play-the-ball will result. The team that had the ball will restart that play from the same tackle count.

Q. What if both teams commit a foul?

Both sports have standard rules around this issue and the referee will determine the appropriate course of action. For example, one team may have stood offside, but if a player on the attacking team commits a professional foul, the referee may choose to 'sin bin' the player and negate the offside call.

Q. What about obstruction?

Once again, both sports are very similar: you cannot run behind your team to gain an advantage. Referees may interpret this rule differently, but as long as the attacking team do not impede the defenders from making tackles, the attack should continue. So, if the officials deem that a defender makes the wrong call, it is play on.

Q. What about fighting?

Rugby Union and Rugby League implement the 'sin bin' and possible send-offs for such offences. Any punches and kicks should result in severe punishments. The game is tough enough already so fighting is uncalled for.

Q. What about professional fouls?

The referee may determine the action. Repeated acts of infringements or deliberate acts to halt that attack may warrant a 'sin bin' or, if continued further, a send-off.

Q. What about stripping of the ball?

The stripping of the ball can only occur in two situations:
1. A one-on-one case between defender and attacker.
2. When the marker is reaching for the ball from a standing position.

Q. What about deliberate knockdowns?

A deliberate knockdown of a pass is allowed unless the ball carrier is still in possession of the ball, in which case it would be deemed an attempted strip. In the case of knocking down a pass, it would not be a 'sin-binning' offence as currently used by Rugby Union.

Q. What about dangerous play?

League and Union apply almost identical interpretations with regards to these matters. However, under a single rugby, the most cautious approach would need to be taken. Many aspects fall into the dangerous play category: fighting, a stiff-arm tackle, a spear (lifting over the horizontal) tackle, trampling a player on the ground, kicking a player, head-butting, eye gouge, shoulder charge to the head, tackling a player with force off the ball or even charging the kicker, or charging into the ruck and losing feet in the process. All these factors may, in accordance with the referee's judgement, result in an automatic send-off. However, if deemed acceptable, the referee, may reduce the penalty to a 'sin bin' offence.

Chapter 8 – The Officials

Q. Who can approach the referee?

Only the designated captain of the team on the field at that time can approach the referee. Also, the referee does not need to stop play to explain rule interpretation and any challenge. Alternatively, if an approach to the referee is considered by that referee to be disrespectful, a penalty such as a 'sin bin' or send-off may result. The simple fact is that all players, officials and fans must respect the authority of the referee.

Q. You keep mentioning a 'sin bin' or send-off. Can you clarify these terms?

These terms may be Australian expressions:
- Yellow card = 'sin bin' (10 minutes off the field)
- Red card = send-off (removed from the game)

Summary of Rules for a United Rugby

For both forms of rugby, there is very little difference in the application of these rules. The following table indicates a summary of which rules would potentially be adopted for the unified game.

Rules of the Game			
Category	Rugby League	Rugby Union	Modified or adopted from both
Players			√
Substitutions			√
Points system	√		
Field markings			√
Lineouts		√	
Scrums		√	
Tackles			√
Referee signals			√
Touch judge signals			√
Offside			√
Forward passes			√
Defensive lines			√
General penalties			√
Foul play			√
Knock-on			√
Kick offs		√	
Line dropouts	√		
Ball dimensions			√
Uniform			√

CHAPTER 9

Domestic Rugby Competitions

Obviously, some significant issues would arise from attempting to create a unified code with regards to local competitions. It is not only the top flight of each domestic league that would need to be addressed but also all the layers underneath. While I acknowledge that this may be a dilemma; however, when broken down, the problem is not as troublesome as it may first appear.

The issue that will prove most challenging is the seasonal difference between League and Union. For the most part, Rugby League has a standard season. In Australia, the game is played during a calendar year in conjunction with the English Super League. Conversely, for Union, the Super Rugby Competition does not align with the competitions in Europe. Compromise in this situation will be critical but before delving into the solution, as a fan, I need to address the matter of prejudice once more.

Rugby League people do not trust 'the Establishment' – consider it to be a part of their DNA. From the very beginning of the split in the game in 1895, and again in the southern hemisphere in 1908, Rugby League came to prominence out of its refusal to buckle to an unfair system. While it took the Establishment 100 years before agreeing to become professional, Rugby League in Australia had established itself as the most dominant form of rugby. In England, Rugby League is cemented in the north. In New Zealand, small pockets have maintained the passion, while in France this issue is of historical note. Regardless, the clubs that make up the game in these nations have built traditions that are valued and are ultimately intertwined into the fabric of the communities they represent.

With this in mind, there may be a chance that Rugby League organisations, particularly in Australia, England, New Zealand and France, will refuse outright any proposals for a merger. This refusal is not based on it not being a good idea but, instead, due to the fact the game has a long memory. For Rugby League, any interactions with the established code rarely have (if ever) been pleasant. The concept of unity may, therefore, be dismissed without consideration due to the fear that it may require 'bending the knee' to a foe it considers to be its persecutor. For many Rugby Union fans, there may be a quiet disbelief about this concept but, nevertheless, feelings of mistrust shape people's actions.

As a consequence, the following information aims to draw this matter to a close. Will every single aspect be addressed? No, of course not. Yet, it may provide a blueprint for a future that allows the opportunity of prosperity and, more importantly, ends the divide between the two codes.

This section attempts to present a country-by-country solution to having a unified competition. It suggests options for the dominant rugby competitions, such as the National Rugby League of Australia, the Super Rugby Competition that affects Australia, New Zealand, South Africa and

Argentina, as well as the English Super League and the English Premiership. Moreover, it highlights possibilities for France's Top 14, America's Major League Rugby and the Pro 14 competition that currently contains teams from Wales, Ireland, Scotland, Italy and South Africa.

National Rugby League and Super Rugby

Australian, New Zealand, South Africa, Argentina and Japan

In both forms of rugby, Australia and New Zealand are dominant figures. In Australia, the National Rugby League prides itself on being an elite sporting competition where, within any year, a new champion can emerge. Meanwhile, in Super Rugby, New Zealand's dominance extends from the national team down to the five franchises that compete. The troubling question here is: *How can the two codes combine if there are two different competitions?*

When Super Rugby started between South Africa, New Zealand and Australia, it surged in popularity – especially in the first two nations. However, Australia, despite having limited success, has struggled to maintain that pressure against the National Rugby League.

Presently, in Super Rugby, there are issues related to the possible break-up of the competition in its current form, with Japan, Argentina and South Africa going their separate ways. Yet, this break-up could potentially produce the best possible outcome – especially for Australia and New Zealand.

Within the NRL, there are 16 clubs. In Super Rugby, New Zealand and Australia have five clubs each. The table on the following page indicates the teams in these two competitions.

No.	National Rugby League	Super Rugby
1	Auckland Warriors (NZ)	Melbourne Rebels
2	Brisbane Broncos	NSW Waratahs
3	Eastern Suburbs Roosters	Queensland Reds
4	Canterbury-Bankstown Bulldogs	ACT Brumbies
5	South Sydney Rabbitohs	Western Force
6	Cronulla-Sutherland Sharks	Auckland Blues
7	Manly-Warringah Sea Eagles	Waikato Chiefs
8	Penrith Panthers	Wellington Hurricanes
9	Parramatta Eels	Canterbury Crusaders
10	Melbourne Storm	Otago Highlanders
11	North Queensland Cowboys	
12	Newcastle Knights	
13	Gold Coast Titans	
14	Canberra Raiders	
15	West Tigers	
16	St George Illawarra Dragons	

Ultimately, the National Rugby League which was formed in 1998 is an extension of the New South Wales Rugby League which was established in 1908. With such a rich history and tradition, this competition would absorb the Super Rugby franchises. And yes, the Super Rugby teams would be invited to join the National Rugby League.

This process would mean that they would become equal partners with the existing NRL clubs and have the same voting rights as those clubs. Moreover, New Zealand Rugby would also have a seat at the table. Together with the NSWRL and the QRL, they would share a position on the commission.

Chapter 9 – Domestic Rugby Competitions

Q. Are you mad? The Australian Super Rugby teams are struggling financially – how could they compete with NRL clubs?

Unfortunately, there would have to be some matters that would need to be addressed – namely financial concerns. However, what price is peace worth? The key here is to ensure as few players, fans and supporters of either code are lost to the game. Adjustments would need to be made, but if the Australian Super Rugby teams could compete, then they should be allowed to. If the Australian Super Rugby clubs weren't able to continue financially, then the fans – for the most part – would accept this fate.

Q. Wait a minute. The NRL already has clubs in Sydney, Brisbane, Melbourne and Canberra – what do the Australian Super Rugby teams add to such competition?

For the invitation to be extended, there would have to be some modification to the Australian Super Rugby teams. If teams meet financial requirements, then the Western Force and Melbourne Rebels would slot straight into the competition and so would the Queensland Reds. The NRL have been looking to add a team to Brisbane for many years and, to a slight extent, have explored options in Perth. Including teams in these markets would mean that there would be a rugby game every week in Brisbane and Melbourne, as well as keeping the rugby fans of Western Australia 'in the loop'. However, it is possible that a branding modification could be applied to the Reds in order to formally assign them as a Brisbane team (Brisbane Reds) and so they were not in competition with the branding of the Queensland Maroons. Additionally, due to the high NRL presence in Sydney, the NSW Waratahs would have to relocate from the Sydney region to the Central Coast. This move would avoid an already overcrowded marketplace and would ensure their presence in the competition was maintained. Lastly, the ACT Brumbies would need to either relocate, merge or fold. In terms of Canberra/ACT, the Canberra Raiders hold sway and, while they are only senior to the Brumbies by roughly fifteen years, the Raiders have a firm hold on the region. For the sake of this proposal, I have suggested that they relocate to Adelaide. The Brumbies moving to Adelaide expands the national footprint while maintaining the club's history and place in a premier competition.

If the Australian Super Rugby franchises had an issue with this, they could either fold or retire to the second division of the state competitions in either the NSW Cup or Queensland Cup. Any team that took the option of folding or withdrawing would split their players between the remaining Australian Super Rugby Franchises.

Q. This is all fanciful, dreamland stuff. You can't be serious?

Yes, it is fanciful and, yes, I am serious. What other way could peace be achieved without one code dominating the other? What way can a united rugby code still exist without alienating fans, players and administrators. The result of cutting teams is losing fans and supporters. The NRL has experienced this and it is an error that should be avoided in the future. Under this proposal, the Super Rugby teams have an equal vote in the progression of the game. They would get to keep their colours, their emblems, their jobs and, most importantly, their place in an elite competition.

Q. What about the New Zealand teams?

The New Zealand franchises would be accepted as they currently are.

Chapter 9 – Domestic Rugby Competitions

Q. With this merger, there would be 26 teams! That's far too many!

Indeed, this proposal recommends a competition that involves 26 teams. That is a lot. However, under this process, no club is sacrificed. No player is left out, no fan is left behind, and no administrator or coach is out of a job. Plus, it provides a complete national rugby competition between Australia and New Zealand.

The setup for the competition would then look as follows:

No.	National Rugby League		
1	Auckland Warriors (NZ)	14	West Tigers
2	Brisbane Broncos	15	St George Illawarra Dragons
3	Eastern Suburbs Roosters	16	Canberra Raiders
4	Canterbury-Bankstown Bulldogs	17	Melbourne Rebels
5	South Sydney Rabbitohs	18	Central Coast Waratahs
6	Cronulla-Sutherland Sharks	19	Brisbane Reds
7	Manly-Warringah Sea Eagles	20	Adelaide Brumbies
8	Penrith Panthers	21	Western Force
9	Parramatta Eels	22	Auckland Blues
10	Melbourne Storm	23	Waikato Chiefs
11	North Queensland Cowboys	24	Wellington Hurricanes
12	Newcastle Knights	25	Canterbury Crusaders
13	Gold Coast Titans	26	Otago Highlanders

Naturally, there would be many issues that would have to be worked out regarding corporate governance and commercial arrangements. Nevertheless, this could be possibly alleviated by establishing a cooling off period whereby previous agreements carry over (to an extent) until new commercial deals are finalised.

A season calendar is most likely to be the easiest solution as that construction is natural for sporting bodies and, therefore, should not be an issue.

The basic premise of a combined Trans-Tasman Competition would involve a 26-week regular season where teams play each other once and then have a bye. The following season, the fixture would reverse.

As evidenced in the following table, the post-season in the modified NRL would consist of 12 teams and would be played over five-weeks.

The entire first week would consist of a straight knockout round between teams ranked 5 through to 12, while teams ranked 1 through to 4 would receive the bye. From the second week moving forward, the post-season would follow the current NRL play-off format.

The teams contesting the Grand Final would be playing for the Proven–Summons trophy.

The table below indicates an exemplar finals schedule.

Week	Round	Fixture
Week 5	Grand Final	**Game 13**: Winner of Game 11 Vs Winner of Game 12
Week 4	Preliminary Final	**Game 11**: Winner of Game 5 Vs Winner of Game 10
		Game 12: Winner of Game 6 Vs Winner of Game 9
		Losers eliminated

Chapter 9 – Domestic Rugby Competitions

Week 3	Semi Final	**Game 9:** Loser of Game 1 Vs Winner of Game 7
		Game 10: Loser of Game 2 Vs Winner of Game 8
		Losers eliminated
Week 2	Qualifying Final	**Game 5:** Team 1 Vs Team 4 – Winner progress to Week 4
		Game 6: Team 2 vs Team 3 – Winner Progress to Week 4
		Game 7: Highest Ranked WC team Vs Lowest Ranked WC team – Loser eliminated
		Game 8: 2nd Highest Ranked WC team Vs 2nd Lowest Ranked WC team – Loser eliminated
Week 1	Wild Card Round	Teams 1 – 4 Bye
		Game 1: Team 5 Vs Team 12 – Loser eliminated
		Game 2: Team 6 Vs Team 11 – Loser eliminated
		Game 3: Team 7 Vs Team 10 – Loser eliminated
		Game 4: Team 8 Vs Team 9 – Loser eliminated

Q. What about South Africa, Argentina and Japan?

Establishing a Trans-Tasman competition would not have a negative impact on Australia or New Zealand but it might have some effect on the nations of Japan, South Africa and Argentina.

The solution for Argentina and Japan is that the clubs from these two nations would simply revert to their domestic competitions.

However, in the case of South Africa, the answer is not as straightforward. But it would be up to the South Africans to decide on whatever pathway is best for them. They could revert to the traditional Currie Cup format or, instead, move to commit their clubs to the Pro 14 League. Once again, that would be a matter for South Africa to determine.

Q. What about all the lower level leagues? Have you considered what the implications for the New South Wales Cup or the Queensland Cup might be? What about the Shute Shield and Queensland Premier Rugby?

Currently, the New South Wales Cup and the Queensland Cup underpin the National Rugby League and act as a pathway for the development of juniors within the game. This system would continue; however, this is not to undermine or weaken the traditions of the Union game. In NSW, the Shute shield is the prominent Rugby Union competition. Therefore, these teams would be invited to participate in the NSW Cup according to their financial stability as well as League requirements. It is unfortunate as it is true, but some of the teams in the Shute Shield occupy the same residential areas as teams that are currently placed in the NSW Cup. As a result, these teams may be placed into a Sydney-based competition that could then serve as a feeder to the NSW Cup.

Moreover, in the case of the current Queensland Premier Rugby teams, they would follow the same path as teams in the Shute Shield. Upon the condition that they satisfy financial regulations, the Queensland Union clubs may be invited into the Queensland Cup. Alternatively, the Union clubs could be incorporated into an elite Brisbane Rugby League competition. This competition could act as one of the many pathway levels for the Queensland Cup.

Q. What about country competitions?

Due to the geographical nature of Australia and the large distance between areas, country football (rugby of either code) is played in groups. The League groups (which are already so well established) would incorporate the Union teams into their corresponding groups – based on geographical location.

Once again, this approach would ensure that no team loses its colours and that no players, coaches, administrators or fans are lost to the game. It is a compromise that would transition the sport into a brighter future.

The Premiership and Super League

England

England is the birthplace of League and Union. England is home to clubs with proud histories, yet, it is also a nation where the divide is as much geographical as it is cultural. The geographic divide is easy to solve; however, the cultural gap is not so easy. Another division is that Rugby Union is played in winter and Rugby League in summer. No doubt, addressing the issues in England would be challenging.

I will discuss the concern of prejudice once more. Rugby League fans would hold much scepticism about a merger and fear that their game would be for better or worse 'taken over' if the two rugby codes were to be combined.

This fear is not without reason – particularly given the fact that English Rugby Union is far wealthier than its League counterpart. However, the governing body scenario is a little different from the issues the clubs face. It is with the clubs that fans should hold hope.

Ultimately, there are three issues to address with the English game:
1. Which teams compete in the top flight and how does the competition work?
2. Which season of the year does the competition run?
3. Which organisation controls the sport?

ISSUE ONE – Which teams compete in the top flight and how does the competition work?

The pyramid system should remain. At present, both competitions have a 12-team top flight. Within the English Super League this consists of 10 English clubs. Under an amalgamated program, the top flight would be a 24-team competition. The top 12 English ranked teams from both codes would join. The second tier would also combine the next 14 highest ranked teams from Union and League and they would then compete in a 28-team competition. Below this level, some more manoeuvring would take place; however, it could be the case that the teams that fall below the top two divisions could combine into a national conference system.

Twenty-four teams in the top flight and twenty-eight teams in the next division are too many!

Usually, I would agree with this statement; however, the teams granted entry into these competitions would have a period of two seasons in their designated competition. In the Premiership, the season would last 23 weeks whereby each team plays each other once. The following year (season 2), the fixture list would be reversed. That way, all teams will have played 46 regular season fixtures over two years. Furthermore, in the case of the Championship, the season would extend for 27 weeks whereby each team plays each other once, reversing the fixture list for the following season to compete in 54 regular season fixtures over two years. After each season, a finals system would be implemented and, as is the case with the NRL, this would consist of a 12-team play-off series.

Q. What would happen after two years?

Following this two-year period, the 14 teams with the highest rank would stay in the top flight for the following season while the bottom ten teams would drop down to the Championship. These ten teams would then be joined by the six teams that were promoted from the level below in order to create a 16-team second tier.

The Final Format: The Pyramid Structure

English Rugby Premiership – 14 teams
The Championship – 16 teams
League One – 16 teams
The National Conference (amateur clubs)

Ultimately, the teams would be placed according to their ranking over the two-year window. If the clubs determined that two years was not enough time to adjust to the variations of the game, then it could be extended to a four-year window, although this would have to be a matter for the clubs to determine.

Q. Wait – I'm confused. Would teams play for two years within their division?

Only in the beginning. The reason for this is simple – change is difficult. By allowing each team two seasons (or possibly four) whereby they play each other team 'home and away' would provide ample opportunity to adapt, sign the required players and coaches, and reduce the chance to fall back on the excuse that a team had an 'off year'.

Q. What about after that initial cycle?

According to their results, the teams would be ranked 1 – 24 (based on the total number of teams). At the end of the initial merged seasons, the competition will be broken into separate divisions (Premiership, Championship and League One). The lowest-ranked clubs will be relegated into a national conference of amateur teams – much like the format currently used with the Football Association of England.

Q. You mentioned play-offs. How would that work in this merged system?

Initially, the play-off structure could work along the same lines as the National Rugby League format that I proposed earlier. The top 12 finals format would apply. It is important to note that, by establishing the play-offs, teams have an opportunity to add to their points tally. Once the pyramid system has been defined, then a top-five finals format would conclude the regular seasons.

I'm confused again.

Here's how I propose the system would be organised. When a team wins a match, they receive two points. If they draw, they receive one point and if they lose, they get nothing. However, as mentioned above, making the play-offs means that teams have a chance to gain bonus points. For every week (with a bye or win) they progress, they get a bonus two points.

The following tables aim to showcase this suggested model. I have incorporated teams that were in the English Super League for the 2019 season, plus the two highest-ranked

Chapter 9 – Domestic Rugby Competitions

English teams from the Championship before the 2020 season shutdown. Also, included are the English Rugby Union Premiership teams.

Bath	Harlequins	Leigh	St Helens
Bristol	Huddersfield	London Irish	Wakefield
Castleford	Hull FC	Northampton	Warrington
Exeter	Hull KR	Sale	Wasps
Featherstone	Leeds	Salford	Wigan
Gloucester	Leicester	Saracens	Worcester

The following table provides a possible Season One ranking.

	Season One				
Rank	Team	Win	Loss	Draw	Points
1	Exeter (MP)	20	3	0	40
2	St Helens	19	4	0	38
3	Saracens	18	5	0	36
4	Wigan	17	6	0	34
5	Gloucester	16	7	0	32
6	Warrington	15	7	1	31
7	Northampton	15	8	0	30
8	Leeds	14	8	1	29
9	Hull FC	14	9	0	28
10	Bath	13	10	0	26
11	Sale	12	11	0	24
12	Wasps	11	12	0	22
13	Bristol	10	13	0	20

14	Wakefield	9	14	0	18
15	Huddersfield	8	15	0	16
16	Harlequins	7	16	0	14
17	Castleford	5	17	1	11
18	Hull KR	5	18	0	10
19	Worchester	4	19	0	8
20	Salford	3	19	1	7
21	Leicester	3	20	0	6
22	Featherstone	2	21	0	4
23	London Irish	1	22	0	2
24	Leigh	0	23	0	0

The top 12 teams would continue into the play-offs.

The Play-off Series could be as shown on the following page.

Chapter 9 – Domestic Rugby Competitions

Season One Play-Off Series

Team	Wild Card	Qualifying Final	Semi Final	Preliminary Final	Grand Final	Bonus Points
Exeter (MP)	Bye Weekend	Win	Bye	Win	Win	12
St Helens		Win	Bye	Win	Loss	8
Saracens		Loss	Loss			2
Wigan		Loss	Win	Loss		4
Gloucester	Win	Loss				2
Warrington	Win	Loss				2
Northampton	Win	Win	Loss			4
Leeds	Win	Win	Win	Loss		6
Hull FC	Loss					0
Bath	Loss					0
Sale	Loss					0
Wasps	Loss					0

Note: MP = Minor Premiers. As a result, they would receive a bonus two points. Every other team would get a bonus two points for wins and byes that have been accumulated during the Play-off Series.

As a consequence, the completed table for Season One would include all points gained throughout the regular and post season.

Season One Completed							
Rank	Team	Win	Loss	Draw	Points	Bonus	Total
1	Exeter	20	3	0	40	12	52
2	St Helens	19	4	0	38	8	46
3	Saracens	18	5	0	36	2	38
4	Wigan	17	6	0	34	4	38
5	Leeds	14	8	1	29	6	35
6	Gloucester	16	7	0	32	2	34
7	Northampton	15	8	0	30	4	34
8	Warrington	15	7	1	31	2	33
9	Hull FC	14	9	0	28	0	28
10	Bath	13	10	0	26	0	26
11	Sale	12	11	0	24	0	24
12	Wasps	11	12	0	22	0	22
13	Bristol	10	13	0	20	NA	20
14	Wakefield	9	14	0	18	NA	18
15	Huddersfield	8	15	0	16	NA	16
16	Harlequins	7	16	0	14	NA	14
17	Castleford	6	17	1	13	NA	13
18	Hull KR	5	18	0	10	NA	10
19	Worchester	4	19	0	8	NA	8
20	Salford	3	19	1	7	NA	7
21	Leicester	3	20	0	6	NA	6
22	Featherstone	2	21	0	4	NA	4
23	London Irish	1	22	0	2	NA	2
24	Leigh	0	23	0	0	NA	0

At the beginning of Season Two, every club would start back on zero points.

Chapter 9 – Domestic Rugby Competitions

The following table presents a possible Season Two ranking.

		Season Two			
Rank	Team	Win	Loss	Draw	Points
1	Saracens	23	0	0	46
2	St Helens	22	1	0	44
3	Wigan	21	2	0	42
4	Gloucester	20	3	0	40
5	Sale	19	4	0	38
6	Hull FC	18	5	0	36
7	Exeter	17	6	0	34
8	Northampton	16	7	0	32
9	Bath	15	8	0	30
10	Wasps	14	9	0	28
11	Leicester	13	10	0	26
12	Hull KR	12	11	0	24
13	Huddersfield	11	12	0	22
14	Castleford	10	13	0	20
15	Bristol	9	14	0	18
16	Featherstone	8	15	0	16
17	London Irish	7	16	0	14
18	Worcester	6	17	0	12
19	Leeds	5	18	0	10
20	Warrington	4	19	0	8
21	Leigh	3	20	0	6
22	Salford	2	21	0	4
23	Wakefield	1	22	0	2
24	Harlequins	0	23	0	0

Please note: I do not realistically think that Leigh and Harlequins would not win any games. These tables are designed to just highlight the example I am attempting to explain.

The top 12 teams would continue into the play-offs.

Season Two Play-Off Series

Team	Wild Card	Qualifying Final	Semi Final	Preliminary Final	Grand Final	Bonus Points
Saracens (MP)	Bye Weekend	Win	Bye	Win	Win	12
St Helens		Win	Bye	Win	Loss	8
Wigan		Loss	Win	Loss		4
Gloucester		Loss	Win	Loss		4
Sale	Win	Win	Loss			4
Hull FC	Win	Win	Loss			4
Exeter	Win	Loss				2
Northampton	Win	Loss				2
Bath	Loss					0
Wasps	Loss					0
Leicester	Loss					0
Hull KR	Loss					0

Note: MP = Minor Premiers. As a result, they would receive a bonus two points. Every other team would get a bonus two points for wins and byes that have been accumulated during the Play-off Series.

Chapter 9 – Domestic Rugby Competitions

As a consequence, the completed table for Season Two would include all points gained throughout the regular and post season.

		Season Two Completed					
Rank	Team	Win	Loss	Draw	Points	Bonus	Total
1	Saracens	23	0	0	46	12	58
2	St Helens	22	1	0	44	8	52
3	Wigan	21	2	0	42	4	46
4	Gloucester	20	3	0	40	4	44
5	Sale	19	4	0	38	4	42
6	Hull FC	18	5	0	36	4	40
7	Exeter	17	6	0	34	2	36
8	Northampton	16	7	0	32	2	34
9	Bath	15	8	0	30	0	30
10	Wasps	14	9	0	28	0	28
11	Leicester	13	10	0	26	0	26
12	Hull KR	12	11	0	24	0	24
13	Huddersfield	11	12	0	22	NA	22
14	Castleford	10	13	0	20	NA	20
15	Bristol	9	14	0	18	NA	18
16	Featherstone	8	15	0	16	NA	16
17	London Irish	7	16	0	14	NA	14
18	Worcester	6	17	0	12	NA	12
19	Leeds	5	18	0	10	NA	10
20	Warrington	4	19	0	8	NA	8
21	Leigh	3	20	0	6	NA	6
22	Salford	2	21	0	4	NA	4
23	Wakefield	1	22	0	2	NA	2
24	Harlequins	0	23	0	0	NA	0

Ultimately, to determine the relegation form for the Premiership, a ranking table would need to be constructed which incorporates all 46 regular season games and play-off games.

The ranking table below presents data that would highlight the completion of two full seasons.

Ranking Table			
Rank	Team	Total Points	Maintained/Relegated
1	St Helens	98	Maintained in the Premiership
2	Saracens	96	
3	Exeter	88	
4	Wigan	84	
5	Gloucester	78	
6	Northampton	68	
7	Hull FC	68	
8	Sale	66	
9	Bath	56	
10	Wasps	50	
11	Leeds	45	
12	Warrington	41	
13	Huddersfield	38	
14	Bristol	38	
15	Hull KR	34	Relegated to the Championship
16	Castleford	33	
17	Leicester	32	
18	Wakefield	20	
19	Worcester	20	
20	Featherstone	20	
21	London Irish	16	
22	Harlequins	14	
23	Salford	11	
24	Leigh	4	

Chapter 9 – Domestic Rugby Competitions

Q. Moving forward, would the promotion-relegation system be applied over a two-year cycle?

As I mentioned earlier, ideally no. Every year following on from this initial stage, the pyramid structure could be used, with a system of promotion and relegation applied.

The Pyramid Structure:

Division 1 – The Premiership
Division 2 – The Championship
Division 3 – League One
National Conference – Top amateur league

Q. So how is the system of promotion and relegation applied?

In the Premiership, a top-five play-off format could be used. The bottom two placed teams will automatically be relegated.

In the Championship and League One, the top placed club would receive an automatic promotion. The next five teams would then compete in a top-five play-off format. For the Championship, the bottom two placed teams will automatically be relegated. For League One, the two lowest-ranked clubs would only get relegated – depending on the financial viability of any amateur teams that are willing to turn professional. Otherwise, there would be no relegation from this level.

Note: Obviously, this concept is just one possible solution. The clubs themselves would naturally be the driving force behind any decisions made in relation to the competition structure.

Q. You haven't discussed the Cup Competitions. What happens to them?

Knockout competitions add an exciting element to the sport. Naturally, with both codes already having knockout competitions of some sort, an aspect of this would be continued over the years.

Firstly, the Rugby League Challenge Cup would be maintained. It is one of the oldest cup competitions in the world and so it would continue to operate but, moving forward, it would include vastly higher numbers. It would, however, be reserved for English teams only.

Secondly, the European Champions Cup would still take place. The numbers of English teams representing the tournament would be a matter for the rugby nations of Europe to agree on.

For any other cup competitions (such as the 1895 Cup or any former Rugby Union Cup competitions), scheduling would be a matter to be addressed in the future by the governing body and clubs.

Q. Which venues would host the relevant club matches?

The location of the Grand Final: Old Trafford Vs Twickenham.

The answer to this question is a little less controversial and would take into account each code's previous business arrangements with their commercial partners. In other words, whatever venues the clubs and the administrators decide on in consultation with their corporate partners.

Q. What about the international teams that make up a part of the Rugby League in England?

The French, Welsh and North American teams would revert to their host nations.

Q. Wait, is that it? There is so much you have not addressed

That is true, but let the clubs decide their fate. Let a fair and equal vote take place and, in that way, a reasonable solution would be achieved. For example:

Chapter 9 – Domestic Rugby Competitions

Should the top flight consist of 12 or 14 teams? Let all the professional clubs vote in a matter that is 1:1. This means that for every Rugby Union club that votes so too does a Rugby League club. If, for any reason, there happens to be more Union clubs than League at the time of the merger and there are only 25 Rugby League club votes, then only 25 Rugby Union votes will take place. This application is fair and equal, and the process removes prejudice, fear and mistrust.

ISSUE TWO – When is the best time to play games?

In the mid-1990s, Rugby League converted to a summer-based season (February–October), while Rugby Union remains a winter-based season (August–June) to this day. Rugby League decided to change their schedule for many reasons; however, this does provide the clubs of the two codes and the two governing bodies a sample from which to make their decision.

This decision would be a matter for professional clubs to decide on. It could be determined that the professional clubs of a united code switch to summer and that the amateur clubs remain in the winter or vice versa. Regardless, when the competition is played should be a matter for the clubs that participate in the game to agree on.

From my own personal bias, I would like to point out that a rugby competition played in the summer season avoids some conflict of interest with the English Soccer Premier League. Also, another issue that should be considered is the weather conditions during which rugby is played. Having a summer rugby season in England will result in fewer games being forfeited due to frozen pitches.

Another positive of shifting rugby games to the summer is that it makes it that much easier to establish an international window for the sport. However, in order to settle the issue of when the season is played, a vote by the clubs linked to the two established competitions would determine the matter.

ISSUE THREE – *Governance*

I admit this detail is lacking here and also throughout the rest of my proposed recommendation to unify rugby codes. No doubt, working through the legalities of such matters would take time, but change is constant and a system where two codes are united presents far more prospects than difficulties. Importantly, in the case of the two English rugby codes, the problems stem from the cultural differences. Without delving too much into the histories of the two sports where deceit and mistrust reign, a fair solution is the only option.

Since the Northern Union broke away from the Rugby Football Union, it seems logical that the Rugby Football League (RFL) should re-join the Union. Yet, re-joining with anything less than equality (for the RFL) can only end one way – a complete and utter failure. The reasons why anything less than equality will fail are many. It stems from the League's relationship with the Establishment. This negative view of the Establishment is deep-seated in the psyches of Rugby League fans in the north of England and across the globe. A lot of the negativity on the part of Rugby League fans and clubs is derived from prejudice, fear and a real lack of trust of Rugby Union. The answer to overcoming this prejudice is complicated but, eventually, a leap of faith needs to be taken. If Rugby League and Rugby Union can come to the table and reasonable people hold court, then a positive outcome should eventuate.

According to my proposal, England Rugby would maintain the governance of the game in England. However, this would not exclude the RFL and its clubs. First, the RFL should be allotted a fair and equal voice at the administration

Chapter 9 – Domestic Rugby Competitions

table of England Rugby. Secondly, where clubs receive a vote in any matters, all Rugby League Clubs would have fair and balanced say on par with their Rugby Union counterparts.

Ideally, the clubs of both codes involved in the Premiership, the Championship and League One should have a far greater say in how their competitions are run, structured and governed. Finally, for any merger of the rugby codes to work in the English game, equity must be established between the clubs and the governing bodies.

The Pro 14

Scotland, Italy, Ireland, Wales and South Africa

The Pro 14 Competition should maintain its current status. Whether or not it should incorporate the South African teams needs to be considered.

If South African teams were to be included, then a possible transition to summer rugby would make more sense – particularly when European teams compete in the southern hemisphere as the climate would be more suitable for playing the game.

If South African clubs were not included in the Pro 14 and South Africa decided to remain with its Currie Cup, a transition by the Pro 14 to summer rugby would still allow for improved playing conditions and would assist in creating an international rugby calendar. Ultimately, any change to either a summer season or remaining in the winter season would have to take place in consultation with the English competition.

Aside from that, given the fact that Rugby League is not dominant in these nations, there would be little to no alteration to their club competition structures at the elite level.

Top 14

France

The Top 14 competition would maintain its current status and Rugby France would keep control of the administration of the game. However, there is a critical element that must be addressed in order for any merger to take place as it is a factor that could (without hesitation) unravel any prospective merger of the codes. Rugby Union in France would need to demonstrate an act of generosity to Rugby League.

For anyone who is currently unaware of the background, persecution of Rugby League has probably been far greatest in France than anywhere else in the world and, as such, the French supporters of Rugby League would be very sceptical and suspicious of any merger.

To counter this issue, an act of generosity could include allowing the Catalan Dragons (currently playing in the English Super League) to spend their first season in the top flight of the French game. From there, merit would determine their position in the league. Secondly, Toulouse Olympique XIII could be inserted into the second tier of the competition structure where performance on the field and finances off the ground would determine its future position. Thirdly, all other French Rugby League teams would need to be appropriately slotted into their equivalent level of competition and, at each level, have equal voting rights as the other Rugby Union clubs in that competition.

The request for equal and fair treatment to a fewer number of League clubs may seem to Rugby Union fans like an unreasonable demand that should be dismissed outright. Conversely, to Rugby League fans who have knowledge of the history, this proposal probably does not go far enough. Unsurprisingly, clubs, administrators and fans can have long

Chapter 9 – Domestic Rugby Competitions

memories which is why I have alluded to the history of the background struggle between the two codes in France.

To elaborate the point but avoid retelling the whole history, there needs to be recognition of the potential for a different mindset between rugby fans. Many Rugby League fans (especially in France) have felt the persecution of the Establishment and, as a result, may have a fixed mindset – one filled with angst and vitriol to their Rugby Union compatriots. Moreover, within League fans is often a deeply rooted belief that, despite their form of the game lacking the popularity of the Union game, the thirteen-a-side version of rugby is by far and away the superior sport and that joining with Union would be a wasteful and pointless exercise. They may consider a merger with Union as 'surrendering to the enemy'.

On the other hand, Union fans dismiss such notions of prejudice and discrimination as ridiculous and claim that Union's global and, in France's case, national popularity proves that it is the superior sport.

If Rugby Union supporters want to dismiss that request then that is fair. However, is allowing clubs a place in a competition where they need to prove their worth on and off the field a harsh request? Especially, if permitting the request would end once and for all the code war between Rugby League and Rugby Union.

To French Rugby League fans, I say this: the fight has been long so now let peace reign. The concept of one united code is beneficial to the clubs, the players, the coaches and the fans far more than maintaining the two separate systems that are continually challenging each other and other sports for players, supporters and sponsors.

Any form of discrimination or prejudice would only continue the animosity between the two codes and their supporters which in the long run is not beneficial to anyone.

Q. So how would the competitions work?

The Catalan Dragons would join the Top 14 for one season. Their maintenance in this competition would depend on their on-field performance as well as their financial sustainability off it.

Toulouse Olympic XIII would join the second tier of French Rugby and, like Catalan, their ability to maintain this role would be dependent on the performance of the team and the economic viability of the club.

Note: Any transition to either playing a summer season or remaining with a winter season would be in consultation with the English competition. I'm aware of the fact that the weather in France – especially the south – contrasts greatly with England so summer rugby may not be feasible. However, the option of a summer rugby season would solve so many international competition structural issues.

Other Leagues of the World

Global Rugby

To start with, Major League Rugby in North America is a significant growth area for both forms of the game. It is a nation with vast numbers of athletes who have the potential to excel in the sport of rugby. Under any merger of the code, Major League Rugby should maintain dominance in the administration of the game in America.

However, the clubs that are currently excluded from the English Rugby League such as the Toronto Wolfpack (and any other North American based Rugby League team) would join the elite level and compete as an equal.

Ideally, the competition would continue on its journey to becoming a permanent fixture on the American sporting landscape.

Chapter 9 – Domestic Rugby Competitions

In other parts of the world where League and Union collide, it will be through mutual negotiation that a governing body would be selected to represent the unified code. To limit the arguments, in most cases this would be the current Rugby Union Board of Control; however, not in all cases. In some countries, Rugby League holds sway and, as such, those governing bodies should assume control of the unified sport.

I note that this may be an area that requires more considerations, but I hold faith that the dominant rugby nations (of both codes) of Australia, England, New Zealand and France would seize the opportunity to assist all other countries to transition into a single rugby entity.

CHAPTER 10

International Rugby

Would you want to watch the Australian Kangaroos vs the New Zealand All Blacks?

Would you love to see the best rugby players Australia has to offer play the best of England at Twickenham?

The process of creating an international fixture list is something both sports regularly undertake. As a consequence, this step is probably the easiest one to achieve. Naturally, if rugby were to merge, there would be some fixture elements that would need to be worked out. Yet, the essential fixtures should remain. The World Cup cycle would not have to end. Likewise, the Great Britain and Ireland Lion tours of Rugby Union would continue, as well as the European Six Nations.

The only scenario that would require adjustment would be if the European nations were to continue playing in winter. Otherwise, the months of October and November could be allocated for any end-of-season tours or international competitions. A mid-year global bracket could be incorporated to allow international competitions between nations in the same region.

Chapter 10 – International Rugby

Whatever the case, at least when different nations play against each other, there is no competing form of rugby on a domestic level that causes any achievements to be diluted.

Australian Kangaroos Vs New Zealand
All Blacks Test Series

In Australia, there is one rugby competition that is the centrepiece of the football calendar. It is State of Origin and it pits the best players Australia has against each other: New South Wales vs Queensland. This sporting masterpiece must continue. At the same time as this event, New Zealand could also play an annual three-match test series against South Africa. If South Africa decide to join in with the European competition, then a tests series could be arranged against Argentina or, alternatively, they could play matches against fellow Pacific countries.

At the conclusion of the State of Origin Series and the All Black matches, a three-test series would be played between Australia and New Zealand. The three-match series would be contested annually. Presently, State of Origin is usually held over five weeks and takes place on Wednesday nights, with a weekend game occurring in the middle. In terms of scheduling, this matter might form part of an international mid-season window. Naturally, a lot would be determined according to whether or not the northern hemisphere reverted to a summer rugby season or remained with the winter schedule.

If the northern hemisphere continued to play matches during their colder months, the Australian and New Zealand series could be played on Wednesday nights following games with the touring teams. Not a perfect solution, however, denying fans the opportunity to see the Kangaroos verses the All Blacks in a unified version of the sport would be 'criminal'.

Q. Hang on! What about the Wallabies and the Kiwis? Both teams have fabulous rugby traditions. Would they not play against each other?

Yes, I agree that both teams do have wonderful rugby traditions and both sides have demonstrated excellence on the field on so many occasions. Nevertheless, it cannot be argued that either team is their nation's prominent rugby team.

To address this matter, the Wallabies would be the name applied to any Australia A team and the Kiwis would be the name applied to any New Zealand A team. These teams would host touring nations during any end-of-season or mid-year tours. More importantly, greater recognition should be given to players who represent these iconic brands, currently and into the future.

For example, when the British and Irish Lions tour, one of their games would be against an Australia A team (The Wallabies) or a New Zealand A team (The Kiwis).

However, if the northern hemisphere switches to a summer rugby season, all tours and tournaments between the northern and southern hemisphere's nations would have to be conducted during October and November each year.

Great Britain and Ireland

Lions Tours and World Cups

Q. You mentioned the Great Britain and Ireland Lions Tours. What about the Rugby League Lions?

Many rugby supporters are unaware that the Lions have been associated with Rugby League since the formation of an international series between Australia. Yet, the magnitude of the Rugby Union version holds sway and incorporates more nations (four-year cycle to Australia, New Zealand, and

Chapter 10 – International Rugby

South Africa). For this reason, the four-year cycle currently employed by the Rugby Union aspect of the Lions should be maintained. However, when the Lions tour in Australia, they would play against the Kangaroos rather than the Wallabies.

Q. Both codes have World Cups so which one should be maintained?

Ideally, a new format would be introduced for World Cups. However, if a compromise is necessary, the Rugby Union World Cup could be selected as the preferred tournament choice. The William Webb Ellis Trophy would still be the trophy lifted by the World Cup winners.

To acknowledge the prestigious element of Rugby League's World Cup (i.e. second oldest World Cup in a team sport), the Paul Barrière Trophy (Rugby League World Cup Trophy) would be the trophy handed to the highest-ranked rugby test nation at the end of a calendar year.

Q. I'm confused. How does the international window work?

First, if both hemispheres were to adopt a February to November game schedule, all end-of-season internationals would take place in October and November. The mid-season fixtures might consist of local internationals, thereby allowing for the Six Nations competition to take place annually, New Zealand to play South Africa in a series and for Australia's State of Origin series to be played. It also would provide time for Australia to play New Zealand during this period.

Q. What if the European nations do not switch to a summer rugby season?

If the European nations don't make the switch to a summer season, then much of what currently occurs in Rugby Union would continue. When Australia and New Zealand travel to Europe or elsewhere, they will do so in October and November whereas European nations would tour at the end of their club season. The problem with this system is that international rugby conflicts with the club competitions of nations. However, it would present opportunities for more international rugby contests.

For example, if a switch did not occur and Great Britain and Irish Lions toured New Zealand, during that calendar year, the All Blacks could play three tests against South Africa, three tests against the Lions and then three tests against Australia before seasons end. Then, after this season was over, they could travel north to play more internationals.

The downside to this suggested model is obvious. Even if all those games were not played, this involves a lot of games and would place a significant demand on the athletes and also rugby clubs. For this reason, the ideal preference would be for rugby to have a common calendar season.

Ultimately, all international schedules would be determined by the governing bodies of each nation and, most importantly, would be drafted in consultations with all clubs that participate in the competitions they represent.

CHAPTER 11

Climbing the Mountain

Located in Asia along the boundaries of China and Pakistan stands defiant a mountain that refuses to yield to anyone. It challenges the will, the passion and the commitment of the climber. More often than not, the harsh conditions of the mountain reign supreme and the climber is defeated.

The peak provides many challenges to the climber and to overcome the obstacles of elevation, the cold and the brutal aspects of nature (all of which squeezes at the lungs and makes a sane mind go mad), hardcore training is required. This training may stretch months but, for many, it takes years of planning, preparation and a life-consuming commitment to the cause.

This mountain is K2. It is the second-highest mountain in the world. While it is not the height of Mount Everest, the challenges and difficulties associated with achieving the climb are unique.

On occasions, K2 is mastered and a willing soul overcomes the dangerous gauntlet and succeeds. The climber has reached the peak. They have achieved their goal, ambition and desire. They have accomplished one of their life dreams. Yet, not a single climber on reaching the summit of the proud and defiant foe declares to the world that they have climbed the biggest mountain in the world! To do so would be foolish.

However, every time the Australian Kangaroos win the Rugby League World Cup, they make that claim. And, likewise, every time the New Zealand All Blacks win the Rugby Union World Cup, they make that same claim.

CHAPTER 12

The Champions

The rampaging boxer beat down on his opponent with a fiery will. His relentless attack forced the weaker fighter to retreat, to gasp for breath and to seek solace in the corner. However, the champion was not going to let the challenger draw breath and pursued his foe like an invading army conquering a rival nation. The defeat was imminent, and despite some resistance by the challenger, he was not going to last the full fifteen rounds. Ultimately, the champion was too fast and too strong. The champion boxer won by a knockout.

The boxer was declared World Champion by the authorities and then raised his fist high in the air and proclaimed with delight, "I am the best fighter in the world!"

Meanwhile, across the ocean, another fight took place in the squared circle. The favourite decimated his opponent landing blow after blow. Yet, like any worthy fighter, the challenger pushed on. He gave it his all. He was fighting for his nation, his family and his honour; yet, defeat was inevitable. In the process of failure, the brawler drew respect from all who understood the nature of the contest.

The authorities handed the winner his belt; he lifted it in the air as the music blasted around the stadium. The lights on the screen said it all, 'World Champion'.

The two boxing bodies oversee the same type of contest with slight variations. There are different round lengths, various scoring systems and unique interpretations of sporting regulations but, ultimately, the two sports are the same. What's more, the two winners, the champions, will never fight against each other.

Isn't that ridiculous?

Conclusion

The expressions that Rugby Union is the game they play in heaven and that Rugby League is the greatest game of all both hold true. For the sport of rugby has all the characteristics required in life. It is tough and uncompromising but requires skill and a dash of flair, as well as bucket loads of resilience in order to provide spectators with a contest that is arguably unparalleled in the modern world.

Nevertheless, despite all the similarities between the codes, I have observed two fundamental differences that may prevent the two sports from uniting.

The first matter relates to two critical rule interpretations:

1. The ruck
2. The numbers of players on the field.

Within this book, I have attempted to explain how each process could work and have gone into detail to explain all the similarities between the two sports.

The second reason why a merger of the two sports could potentially fail is due to cultural differences and the sense of prejudice that plague both sets of supporters and administrators.

The issue of prejudice is tough to overcome, and I do note my lack of persuasive skills. For this reason, I have tried to be as unbiased and reflective as possible within this book. There is no reason for the two sports to continually battle against each other for fans, participants and revenue. Having attended multiple State of Origin and Grand Final matches in the past, I have personally witnessed the greatness of both codes. Likewise, I was present when, in 2001, the Australian Wallabies defeated the Great Britain and Irish Lions and also defeated the All Blacks for the Bledisloe Cup. Both sports offer excitement, yet, I keep coming back to the same point: neither code can claim that they are the best rugby organisation in the world.

The naysayers will also argue that I have not given enough consideration to all the smaller Rugby (League and Union) nations around the world. This is true; I do not deny this; however, I do suggest (and reinforce my point) that with any progression to a single code, a thorough process of consultation should take place. I have indicated that the rugby powerhouse nations of Australia, England, France and New Zealand could act as negotiators and guides for such matters. The reason why I have tended to focus on the rugby superpowers is simple – it is because rugby (League or Union) are very popular sports for these countries and failure to get these nations to engage in peace and unity is to result in failure of any concept of a single code. These nations would be the lead countries that would determine (through funding and influence) the future of either code.

Additionally, I have provided templates for merged competitions in Australia and New Zealand, England, France and the other nations that compete in the Pro 14 league. These competitions were presented to showcase how much stands to be gained as a result of a merged code.

Conclusion

In conclusion, the following points will need to be addressed in order to unify the code of League and Union into one single sport:
1. Rules of the game
2. Domestic competitions
3. International Rugby

Naturally, there is a whole range of other obstacles: corporate governance, finance and junior pathways. I have not managed to cover every aspect of this subject here. Yet, what I hope I have achieved as a result of this book is to ensure that the door is opened and the path is cleared to creating a unified sport. In this way, for those who are brave, the journey that awaits will not be one fraught with doubt but, if ventured, will be one of enjoyment.

In any case, I admit my proposal for unifying Rugby League and Rugby Union into a single sport is purely hypothetical. If nothing eventuates from this book, then that is fine. I will continue to enjoy Rugby League / Union for all the skill and excitement that they offer me.

To sign off, I would ask that you consider the following points:

For all Rugby players – League and Union:

Don't you want to compete against the best?

For the all Rugby Union fans where League currently has no claim or dominance:

If you could see your nation play against another opponent that was equal or quite possibly superior to the All Blacks, would you want to watch the match?

For the English fans:

If St Helens or Wigan were to play Saracens or Exeter – would you watch the match?

For the Aussies and Kiwis:

If the Australian Kangaroos were to play the New Zealand All Blacks – would you watch the match?

For all Rugby fans:

Do you want to see the best rugby players competing in the same sport?

If you answered, yes, you agree that a unified code is the best way forward for the game of rugby.

Recommended Reading List

Books

Collins, T. (2006). *Rugby League in Twentieth Century Britain: A Social and Cultural History*. Routledge.

Collins, T. (2006). *Rugby's Great Split: Class, Culture and the Origins of Rugby League Football* (2nded.). Routledge.

Rylance, M. (1999). *The Forbidden Game: The Untold Story of French Rugby League*. League Publications Ltd.

Websites

Australian Rugby – https://www.rugby.com.au/
Fédération Française de Rugby – https://www.ffr.fr/
Guinness PRO14 – https://www.pro14.rugby/
International Rugby League – https://intrl.sport/
Major League Rugby – https://www.majorleague.rugby/
National Rugby League – https://www.nrl.com/
New Zealand Rugby – https://www.nzrugby.co.nz/
Rugby Football League – https://www.rugby-league.com/
Rugby Football Union – https://www.englandrugby.com
SANZAAR Super Rugby – https://super.rugby/superrugby/
World Rugby – https://www.world.rugby

Acknowledgements

Nothing is accomplished without support and this book holds true to this notion. It would not have been possible for me to have published this book without feedback and guidance offered by Kirsty Ogden. Her insights and suggestions about the manuscript proved to be invaluable.

Also, it would be remiss of me not to offer my heartfelt thanks to all my friends and family who offered me their unconditional support throughout the writing process.

About the Author

Mark Campbell was born in Sydney, New South Wales. He grew up in a family of Rugby League fans and the game and the South Sydney Rabbitohs became his obsession, his passion, and his religion. Later in life, Mark developed a respect for the game of Rugby Union but League has remained his first love.

Mark would like to see the end of the 'code war' between the two sports. Most importantly, he hopes the ideas that he has put forward in this book will resonate with those people with the vision, imagination and the capacity to see the benefits associated with creating one unified form of rugby.

www.ingramcontent.com/pod-product-compliance
Lightning Source LLC
Chambersburg PA
CBHW051539010526
44107CB00064B/2778